MW00561752

THE PSYCHOSOCIAL EXPERIENCES OF

RETIRED
POLICE OFFICERS

A Phenomenological Study by
DR. STEVEN M. KELSEY

Dissertation Submitted in Partial Fulfillment
of the Requirements for the Degree of
Doctor of Philosophy
Forensic Psychology

WALDEN UNIVERSITY
01/01/2022

Copyright © 2022 Dr. Steven M. Kelsey. *All rights reserved.*

ISBN 978-1-66786-530-0 (Print)

ISBN 978-1-66786-531-7 (eBook)

No part of this publication may be reproduced, distributed, or transmitted in any form or by any means, including photocopying, recording, or other electronic or mechanical methods, without the prior written permission of the author, except in the case of brief quotations embodied in critical reviews and certain other noncommercial uses permitted by copyright law.

Abstract

This phenomenological study was conducted to deeply explore retired police officers' perceptions of their retirement along with factors that positively or negatively affect their retirement. This issue is critical to explore to ensure that officers receive the support they need to transition out of their career into retirement positively and manage some of the emotional turmoil that have been seen to result from retirement (e.g., denial, stress, anger, anxiety). Major challenges reported by officers included feeling powerless to help others, being unable to contribute, and losing their self-identity. Benefits included more time and less stress, provided they were emotionally, mentally, and financially prepared. Many reported missing their job. This reinforces previous research and development of theory related to role identity. Financial security was an important factor as well that helped the retirement go smoothly. Involuntary retirement was associated with poor mental health outcomes and feelings of abandonment. Officers who were well-prepared to retire and doing so voluntarily had many positive experiences as they retired, largely connected to proadaptive behavior. Missing the experience of being an officer, missing coworkers, and no negative experiences were reported by the participants, which is somewhat novel as previous research has focused on negative outcomes related to retirement. Proadaptive behavior that ensures financial security and emotional readiness for retirement as findings of this work should be of interest to law enforcement agencies.

Dedication

This dissertation is dedicated to all of the spiritual leaders who have mentored me. To the late Bishop C.L. Morton Jr. of Detroit Michigan: although you called me your son, I felt like a student. I was the one who was learning. To Lady Yvonne Morton (Mom): thank you! I also dedicate this work to my grandfather, Dr. O.W. McClain, who first taught me the value of education and critical thought.

Acknowledgments

First and foremost, I am extremely grateful to my Chair and Second Chair, Dr. Matthew Geyer, and Dr. Beth Walters, for their invaluable advice, continuous support, and patience during my PhD study. Their immense knowledge and plentiful experience have encouraged me in my academic research and daily life. I would also like to thank the faithful leadership of Spirit Filled New Life Church Ministries. I would like to thank all the leadership of Alpha and Omega Church Ministries International, Inc. It is their kind help and support that have made completing my study a wonderful time. Finally, I would like to express my gratitude to my mother, Erma Jean Rice, my wife, Diane E. Kelsey, and my children. Whitney, Amaris and Josiah. And the arrival of my First granddaughter Jurnee Without their tremendous understanding and encouragement in the past few years, it would have been impossible for me to complete my study.

Table of Contents

List of Tables

CHAPTER 1:

Introduction to the Study

Retirement is considered a major milestone that could affect psycho-social functioning (Eagers et al., 2018). Even though most individuals generally have positive experiences during retirement (Syse et al., 2015), police officers can be at risk for less adaptive transition given the nature of their work (Bullock et al., 2018). In this study, I explored how retired police officers perceived their psychosocial experiences during their retirement and the positive and negative factors that impacted their retirement. The potential social implication of this study is the development of interventions that can help police officers become more positively adjusted in their retirement based on a deeper understanding of their psychosocial experiences.

In this chapter, I provide an overview of the study. The background section will provide the foundation for the research problem, purpose of the study, and the research questions. The conceptual framework, which is grounded in continuity theory and role theory, will also be discussed. A brief description of the nature of the study, which is qualitative phenomenological design, will also be made. Key definitions, assumptions, scope and delimitations, and limitations will also be discussed. The significance of the study for scholars and practitioners will also be included in the discussion. The chapter ends with a summation of the most pertinent aspects of the proposed research study.

Background

Compared to other occupations or job roles, many police officers are often exposed to a high number of stressful situations (Leppma et al., 2018;

Marchand et al., 2015). Regardless of context, law enforcement officers are routinely exposed to traumatic incidents, violence, or confrontations (Price, 2017). Due to this exposure, law enforcement officers are considered high-risk for developing physical and psychological health problems (Steinkopf et al., 2015). Some of these possible issues include depression, alcohol abuse, trauma, and stress-related disorders (Price, 2017). Despite conflicting results about the rate of suicides among law enforcement officers, Violanti et al. (2018) found domestic abuse and alcohol abuse are common precursors among law enforcement officers who committed suicide.

Compulsory retirement, as opposed to voluntary retirement, is potentially problematic given that research studies have generally indicated that involuntary retirement is associated with more negative experiences and outcomes (Cameron & Griffiths, 2016; Rhee et al., 2016). For instance, researchers such as Rhee et al. (2016) found that involuntary retirement is negatively associated with mental health problems as a result of less perceived control of the retirees' finances. Moreover, involuntary retirement among law enforcement officers can result in low moods and feelings of isolation and abandonment, which can negatively affect their self-report of life satisfaction (Cameron & Griffiths, 2016).

Research on the transition to retirement has generally indicated that retirees are able to maintain their well-being during retirement (Henning et al., 2016; Syse et al., 2015). Despite this, a few studies contradicted this finding, indicating depressive symptoms tended to be higher among retired individuals who belong in lower occupational class backgrounds compared to those who are still employed (Shiba et al., 2017). The transition to retirement can be influenced by various factors (van den Bogaard et al., 2016). This implies that there are certain contextual and individual factors that can determine whether an individual will have a positive or negative experience during their retirement (Henning et al., 2016; Syse et al., 2015; van den Bogaard et al., 2016)

The transition to retirement is a complex life milestone, underscoring the importance of engaging in preretirement planning and preparation

(Eagers et al., 2018; van den Bogaard et al., 2016). Preretirement conditions such as physical job demands and psychological job stresses can be important factors that can affect the experiences of retirees (van den Bogaard et al., 2016). More specifically, those who have psychologically stressful jobs are more likely to experience gains during their retirement, but those with physically demanding jobs will not experience the same self-rated health gains (van den Bogaard et al., 2016).

Retirees generally experience positive emotions and well-being during retirement, often having better self-reported mental health perceptions compared to individuals who are still in the workforce (Syse et al., 2015). This is not universal, however, and the psychological experiences of some retirees can be replete with negative emotions. Denial, stress, depression, anger, and anxiety are some of the common psychological experiences of retirees (Abdulkadir et al., 2018; Burkert & Hochfellner, 2017; Saraswat, 2017; Shiba et al., 2017; Topa & Valero, 2017).

Another aspect of the functioning of retirees that can be affected is their social relationships, given that these relationships play an important role in the successful transition of many retirees (Haslam et al., 2018). The social experiences of retirees can be characterized by perceived social isolation (Burkert & Hochfellner, 2017). Many retirees, including police officers, lose their social support during their retirement (Hope, 2017). Hence, many retirees continue to engage in work that is related to their main career or pursue a bridging job (Dingemans et al., 2017). This behavior is not necessarily always motivated by the increased need for financial income, but the continued need for social interaction with other people (Dingemans et al., 2017).

There was a gap in the literature because no previous studies address how retired police officers perceive their psychosocial experiences during their retirement and the positive and negative factors that can impact their retirement. Through my qualitative phenomenological study, I provided an understanding of the different psychosocial challenges that retired police officers experience during retirement. Prior research has largely focused

3

on quantitative studies, which has helped to identify some of the limitations in the literature. However, a qualitative study allowed for an in-depth understanding of how some of the known factors are actually experienced in individuals, how these factors interact, and how additional unknown factors may contribute to the retirees' lived experiences. The information obtained from the semistructured interviews addressed the gap in research of the lived experience of police officers during retirement. This is important because previous research has primarily lacked in-depth details of this phenomenon. This study can also be instrumental in the development of interventions that can help police officers become more positively adjusted in their retirement based on a deeper understanding of their psychosocial experiences. The results of the study can also be used as the foundation for future research on the psychosocial experiences of retired police officers.

Problem Statement

The problem that I addressed in my study was the lack of information surrounding how retired police officers perceive their psychosocial experiences during their retirements and the positive and negative factors that impact their retirements. It is not uncommon for police officers to experience psychosocial difficulties during their retirement (Bullock et al., 2018). Denial, stress, anger, and anxiety are common psychosocial effects of retirement among many retirees (Abdulkadir et al., 2018). These psychosocial difficulties during retirement, particularly among former police officers, are poorly understood because no previous researchers have delved into the in-depth experiences and perceptions of those police officers who are already in their retirement (Bullock et al., 2018).

Retirement is considered a major life change for emergency service personnel, underscoring the need to understand the psychological challenges experienced by police officers during retirement (Bracken-Scally et al., 2016). Police officer retirement is characterized by a multi-dimensional process that is influenced by the circumstances of their retirement (Bullock et al., 2018). Even though mandatory retirement gives police officers the opportunity to plan out their retirement, many do not engage in active preparation for this life transition (Abdulkadir et al., 2018).

Well-being and life satisfaction are important adjustment facilitators for the successful transition to retirement (Wetzel et al., 2016). The successful transition of police officers is also predicted by career success, leisure satisfaction, and quality of health; however, these relationships are mediated by the presence and quality of social support (Umukoro & Adejuwon, 2017). Many police officers lose their social support during their retirement (Hope, 2017). Police officers are also known for avoiding mental health services as a result of their fear of being stigmatized (Bullock & Garland, 2017). Addressing these psychosocial issues during retirement in a qualitative study was necessary in order to gain a deeper understanding of how police officers can be better prepared for retirement (Bullock et al., 2018).

Purpose of the Study

The purpose of this phenomenological study was to explore how retired police officers perceive their psychosocial experiences during their retirement and the positive and negative factors that impact their retirement. Given that I sought to understand retired police officers based on their own internal meaning of the phenomena, a qualitative phenomenological study was the most appropriate and optimal research design (Moustakas, 1994). Through this study, I gained an understanding of the different psychosocial challenges that retired police officers experience during retirement. The findings of this study can also be instrumental in the development of interventions that can help police officers become more positively adjusted in their retirement based on a deeper understanding of their psychosocial experiences.

Research Questions

Based on the problem identified from the literature review and the corresponding purpose statement, the research questions (RQ) of the study are the following:

RQ1: How do retired police officers perceive their own psychosocial experiences during their retirement?

RQ2: What factors positively impact the retirement of police officers?

RQ3: What factors negatively impact the retirement of police officers?

Conceptual Framework

The conceptual framework of this study was informed by the integration of the theory of continuity (Atchley, 1989) and the role theory of retirement (Mead, 1913). The theory of continuity was appropriate for the study because of the insights gained regarding the tendency of retirees to adopt a way of life that is similar to their way of life before retirement (Atchley, 1989). My selection of role theory was also appropriate for the study because of the importance placed on the perspectives of individuals in understanding their experiences and adjustments during retirement. Both continuity theory and role theory were used in the study to inform the understanding of the lived experience of retired police officers regarding their transition to retirement.

The main tenet of the continuity theory is that retirees are more likely to experience psychological well-being when they are able to preserve a lifestyle that is somewhat similar to their life before retirement (Atchley, 1989). Through adaptive choices, middle-aged and older adults are preserving and maintaining both internal and external structures that are tied to their past experiences and social environment. Based on continuity theory, change—such as retirement—is seen as related to the perceived past of a person, facilitating the continuance of behaviors and psychological beliefs that are central to one's preretirement functioning (Atchley, 1989).

Continuity theory has been used as framework for other studies involving retirement (Henning et al., 2016; Oleksiyenko & Życzyńska-Ciołek, 2018). For instance, Henning et al. (2016) used continuity theory to frame their review of previous longitudinal studies to understand the well-being of retirees during retirement, which was influenced by their ability to transition successfully in this phase of life. Oleksiyenko and Życzyńska-Ciołek (2018) also used continuity theory to support their hypothesis that retired employees were likely to engage in activities that were congruent to the activities they were exposed to during their active working years.

Another theoretical component of my study's conceptual framework was role identity theory, wherein the concepts of self and the mind are considered the foundation (Mead, 1913). Specifically, roles are developed through social interaction as perceived and interpreted by individuals as the actors (Mead, 1913). Wetzel et al. (2016) framed retirement as a short-term change in status and a long-term development of new routines based on the current resources of the retiring individuals. Using the unique experiences and perceptions of individuals, role identity theory underscores the importance of developing a new role identity that would assist in offsetting the loss of the former role identity as a result of retirement (Henning et al., 2016).

Role theory has also been used as framework for understanding the psychosocial experiences of retirees and older individuals (Henning et al., 2016; Leedahl et al., 2017; van Ingen & Wilson, 2017). For instance, Leedahl et al. (2017) used role theory to frame how nursing home residents could benefit from civic participation because it gives them a role to assume during retirement, countering the role losses from their previous employment. Van Ingen and Wilson (2017) also used role identity theory to justify their hypothesis that many retirees will choose to volunteer in order to assume another role identity during their retirement. These research studies underscore the importance of having a newly acquired role in the transition of retirement in order to facilitate a more successful transition. Role theory was used in the study to inform the understanding of the lived experiences of retired police officers regarding their transitions to retirement. Using both of these theories allowed for a deeper understanding and interpretation of the findings in a more meaningful way that could not otherwise have been accomplished if only one theory was used.

Nature of the Study

Phenomenological research was used to understand the lived experiences of retired police officers regarding their transitions to retirement, perceptions of their changing roles, any psychological problems and difficulties experienced during this period, and the positive and negative experiences that impact their retirement. Phenomenological research is the systematic exploration of the lived experience of individuals, which is subjective in nature (Moustakas, 1994). It is focused on interpreting the internal experiences of a group of individuals as a method of understanding a complex phenomenon.

A phenomenological research study was consistent with studying the lived experience and informed perceptions of retired police officers. The selection of phenomenological research design was appropriate because the exploration of the lived experience of retired police officers required me to interpret the officers' own subjective perspectives and views on retirement. Other groups of individuals, such as the officers' spouses or parents, would not have been able to provide the relevant internal processes that are required to understand the lived experiences and informed perceptions of retired police officers.

The phenomenon that I explored in my study was the psychosocial experiences of police officers during their retirement. The key concepts that I explored in this study were retirement, the psychosocial factors that define the experiences of former police officers during this phase in their lives, and the positive and negative aspects that affected their retirement. The unit of analysis was at the individual level, where I focused on the subjective experiences of each retired police officer who participated in the study.

The sample consisted of 10 retired police officers in a large city in a northeastern state in the United States. I used individual semistructured interviews to collect data, which gave me the opportunity to be flexible and probe for additional relevant information from each participant without being constrained by a strict format or guide (Chan et al., 2013). To answer the research questions of the study, I utilized an interpretive phenomeno-logical analysis (IPA) methodology; the goal of the IPA is to capture the essence of the experiences of the participants by developing themes from the data (Smith, 2014).

Definitions

I used many key terms and concepts throughout this study. I com-piled a complete list of these terms and concepts and their definitions below.

Compulsory retirement. Compulsory retirement is an involuntary retirement forced by the employer (Abdulkadir et al., 2018).

Mandatory retirement. Mandatory retirement refers to a predeter-mined type of retirement wherein employees are forced to leave their jobs because they have reached a certain age (Abdulkadir et al., 2018).

Retirement. Retirement refers to the process wherein an employee exits the workforce (Wang & Wanberg, 2017).

Psychosocial. Psychosocial refers to the different psychological and social factors relevant to the experiences of individuals (Haslam et al., 2018)

Voluntary retirement. Voluntary retirement pertains to early retirement that is initiated by an employee or an employer (Abdulkadir et al., 2018).

Assumptions

Assumptions are relevant factors within a study that are assumed to be true even if no explicit evidence exist to support them (Simon & Goes, 2013). One assumption I had while completing this study was that all par-ticipants would be honest when providing answers to the questions in the semistructured interview. The reason why this assumption was necessary in the context of the study was that there was only one data source, there was only a small number of participants, and no quantitative checks were conducted to detect deception in responses.

Another assumption I had during this study was that 10–14 partic-ipants were adequate to generate themes that illuminate the psychosocial experiences of police officers who are in retirement. One reason why this assumption was necessary in the context of the study was that the sample size was small so that I could engage in prolonged contract with the participants and gain a deeper understanding of their experiences. Another reason why this assumption was necessary was that data saturation is often used by other researchers to determine that the sample size is sufficient to generate themes (Francis et al., 2010).

Scope and Delimitations

Scope and delimitations pertain to the factors within a study that researchers have control over (Simon & Goes, 2013). One delimitation of this study was that the scope was defined by the psychosocial experiences of police officers who have already retired voluntarily. I chose this specific focus because of the indication in the literature that voluntary and nonvoluntary retirees generally had different experiences and challenges (Cameron & Griffiths, 2016; Rhee et al., 2016). By focusing only on those former police officers who voluntarily retired from the police force, I was able to capture the unique experiences of this homogenous group.

My study was also bounded to the population of retired police officers in a northeastern state in the United States. Because of the economic, political, and social contexts, the results of my study may not be transferable to police officers outside of this region. Additionally, the conceptual framework was bounded by the lens of the theory of continuity (Atchley, 1989) and the role theory of retirement (Mead, 1913). This means that both theories provided context for the study and the interpretation of the findings were based on the relevant principles of these two theories.

Given these delimitations and the scope of the bounded exploration, the transferability of the study is confined to the psychosocial experiences of retired police officers whose retirement was voluntary and whose work was in the northeastern region of the United States. This means that my findings are not outside of the bounded sample characteristics. The results may only be transferred if enough similarities exist between the particulars of my study and the target group where the findings are intended to be used.

Limitations

Limitations are the uncontrollable factors within a study that pose possible weakness or bias that could affect the study's transferability or dependability (Simon & Goes, 2013). The limitations related to design and methodological weaknesses of my study included subjectivity of the data and the relative complexity of the data analysis procedure. I strictly followed the guidelines set by Smith (2014) about interpretive phenomenological analysis.

Limitations of transferability and dependability included the inability to generalize the findings to all retired police officers. Given the experiential differences in voluntary and nonvoluntary retirement (Cameron & Griffiths, 2016; Rhee et al., 2016), the results of my study may not be transferable to police officers who retired either mandatorily or compulsorily. The results may not be transferrable outside the current study at all if not enough similarities exist in terms of the sample composition, characteristics of the context, or the nature of the phenomenon.

Furthermore, researcher bias could have influenced the research findings had I not been able to successfully set aside my preconceived ideas about the psychosocial experiences of retired police officers. This potential bias was addressed by engaging in the psychological process of bracketing during data collection and analysis. According to Tufford and Newman (2012), bracketing in qualitative studies has the potential to prevent the negative influence of preconceptions that could pollute the quality of the study process.

Significance

One contribution of this phenomenological research study was that advance knowledge in the discipline included the enhanced understanding of the different psychosocial challenges that retired police officers experience during retirement. I was also able to understand the relevance of roles and transitions during retirement. The information obtained from the semistructured interviews addressed the gap in research of the lived experience of police officers during retirement, given that previous research has lacked in-depth details of this phenomenon.

The potential contributions of the study that advance practice and policy include better preretirement programs for police officers that better prepare them for their psychosocial adjustment. This research study can also be instrumental in the development of interventions that help police officers become more positively adjusted in their retirement based on a deeper understanding of their psychosocial experiences. As a result of the findings of this research study, the leaders of police departments could be encouraged to be more proactive with their assistance towards retiring police.

The potential implications for positive social change that are consistent with and bounded by the scope of the study include better psychosocial adjustment of retired police officers. When retired police officers are better adjusted to their retirement, common psychosocial problems such as denial, social isolation, stress, anger, and anxiety may be lessened or avoided (Abdulkadir et al., 2018). The workload of the health care systems may be lessened if police departments are proactive in putting programs in place that facilitate better transitions to retirement for their police officers. The results of my study may have also directly benefited the participants by helping them to learn more about themselves, thus contributing to positive social change on the individual level in their own community.

Summary

The transition to retirement is a complex life milestone for any individual, often characterized by significant changes in a person's psychosocial experiences (Eagers et al., 2018; van den Bogaard et al., 2016). Through this study, I addressed the lack of information about how retired police officers perceive their psychosocial experiences during their retirement and the positive and negative factors that impact their retirement. The purpose of my phenomenological study was to explore how retired police officers perceive their psychosocial experiences during their retirements and the positive and negative factors that impact their retirements.

The conceptual framework of this phenomenological study were informed by the integration of the theory of continuity (Atchley, 1989) and the role theory of retirement (Mead, 1913). The theory of continuity was appropriate for the study because of the insights gained regarding the tendency of retirees to adopt a way of life that is similar to their way of life before retirement (Atchley, 1989). The selection of role theory was appropriate for the study because of the importance placed on the perspectives of individuals in understanding their experiences and adjustment during retirement. Using both of these theories allowed me to gain a deeper and more meaningful understanding and interpretation of the findings that could not otherwise have been accomplished if only one theory was used.

The sample consisted of 10 retired police officers in a large city in a northeastern state in the United States. Individual semistructured interviews were used to collect data, which gave me the opportunity to be flexible and probe for additional relevant information with each participant without being constrained by a strict format or guide (Chan et al., 2013). To answer the research questions of the study, I developed themes needed to capture the essence of the experiences of the participants using the IPA methodology (Smith, 2014). The next chapter is a detailed review of the literature on the retirement of police officers and the different psychosocial experiences and challenges during retirement.

CHAPTER 2:

Literature Review

The problem that I addressed in this study was that many police officers experience psychosocial difficulties during retirement (Bullock et al., 2018). While researchers have lent insight into some of the various challenges associated with retirement among police officers (Bullock & Garland, 2017), there remained a lack of research on the lived experiences and psychosocial state of police officers during retirement. In response to the aforementioned problem and research gap, the purpose of this qualitative phenomenological study was to explore how retired police officers perceive their psychosocial experiences during their retirements.

This chapter consists of a review of extant literature that is relevant to the topic of my study. To locate articles for this review, Google Scholar and EbscoHost research databases were used. The search terms *retirement, police retirement, retiring from police work, police retirement antecedents, police retirement success factors, predictors of retirement experiences, determinants of retirement experiences, retirement experiences, retirement challenges, role theory police work, role theory police retirement, bridge employment, gradual employment, bridge employment determinants, predictors of bridge employment, retirement theory of continuity,* and *theory of continuity police retirement* were utilized to locate relevant literature.

The theoretical framework of this study, which consisted of the theory of continuity and the role theory of retirement, is discussed first within the context of the current study. Subsequently, I explore the nature of retiring from police work, including commonly-cited antecedents and challenges. A summary concludes this chapter.

Theoretical Framework

The theoretical framework of this research is comprised of the theory of continuity and role theory of retirement. Continuity theory describes how older adults transitioning to retirement tend towards habits and actions that preserve both external and internal life structures from their life before retirement; retirees who preserve aspects of their lifestyle before retirement are more likely to experience psychological well-being during and after the transition (Atchley, 1989). Through adaptive choices, middle-aged and older adults preserve structures associated with past experiences and social environments (Atchley, 1989). For this reason, a perspective based in continuity theory emphasizes the importance of one's degree of preparedness for retirement; individuals who choose to retire on their terms and not due to compulsory retirement, health concerns, and other challenges frequently have more time to prepare and ensure continuity between their pre- and postretirement lifestyles (Bullock et al., 2019).

Many researchers have used continuity theory to frame studies on the transition to retirement and how retirees adjust to the change (Henning et al., 2016; Oleksiyenko & Życzyńska-Ciołek, 2018). Henning et al. (2016) used the continuity theory to frame their review of previous longitudinal studies to understand the processes of change and continuity experienced by retirees during retirement. The researchers found that while most retirees maintain the same level of well-being after retiring, experiences vary significantly across certain demographics, with some subgroups noting substantial challenges and a sense of loss. Further, adaptive actions seemed to mediate retirement-transition experiences (Henning et al., 2016). One adaptive action some retirees take is decreasing their amount of work gradually or taking occasional jobs following retirement. Oleksiyenko and Życzyńska-Ciołek (2018) also utilized a continuity theory framework and found support for the notion that retirees often engage in their same preretirement activities, with some taking occasional or part-time work to ease the transition.

Role identity theory is the second component of the theoretical framework. The concepts of the self and the mind are central to role identity theory (Mead, 1913). Individuals develop their identities and roles through social interaction and their perceptions of social interactions (Mead, 1913). Further, individuals' perceptions of their roles can change and shift over time in response to new experiences, responsibilities, and routines. From a role theory perspective, retirement is viewed as a short-term change in status and a long-term development of new routines based on factors at the individual level, such as personal resources, social networks, and health. Examining retirement from a role identity theory perspective underscores the importance of developing a new role identity after transitioning to retirement that helps to offset the loss of one's role identity before retirement (Henning et al., 2016). Despite this, it is important to note that the degree to which retirees feel a sense of loss when transitioning out of their working role can be significantly impacted by the nature of one's preretirement occupation. In particular, individuals working in law enforcement and other fields characterized by a prominent sense of group membership frequently feel a more significant sense of identity-related loss when transitioning to retirement than individuals working in more solitary environments or those that are not team-based (Charman, 2017).

Numerous researchers have analyzed the psychosocial experiences of retirees and older individuals from a role identity theory perspective (Leedahl et al., 2017; van Ingen & Wilson, 2017). A quantitative analysis conducted by Leedahl et al. (2017) revealed that civic engagement was significantly beneficial to the well-being of nursing home residents. The researchers suggested that nursing home residents benefit from civic participation because it can be a source of social support that gives them a sense of group membership and a role to assume during retirement. Van Ingen and Wilson (2017) also used the role identity theory to frame the exploration of the identities and well-being of retirees. Among a sample of 572 philanthropic volunteers who were older than 50, the researchers found that the role identity associated with volunteer work was more significant to individuals as they aged and settled into their postretirement lifestyle (van Ingen & Wilson, 2017).

Findings from relevant role identity theory research studies underscore the significance of acquiring new roles and facets of identity as retirees transition from their active working role into a retired role. Continuity theory, then, reinforces the importance of retirees maintaining some degree of similarity when transitioning from working to retirement to avoid negative retirement outcomes. Throughout my study, I used these theories to frame my exploration of retirees' perspectives on their experiences and adjustment during retirement, as well as many retirees' tendency to adopt a new lifestyle that is similar to their preretirement lifestyle. I utilized both theories utilized as a framework for understanding the lived experiences of retired police officers and the nature of their transition to retirement.

Review of the Literature: Transitioning from Work to Retirement

This section centers on the process of transitioning from a working role to retirement. Subtopics of discussion include factors that influence the transition, types of retirement, and the nature of the transition. In one subsection, I focus on a discussion of working after retirement in a part-time or volunteer capacity.

The nature of transitioning from a working role to retirement is complex and multifaceted. Research on this transition has revealed significantly different experiences, both positive and negative. The type of retirement one undergoes can significantly impact the trajectory of the process (Cameron & Griffiths, 2016; Rhee et al., 2016). Retirement can be voluntary, compulsory, or mandatory (Abdulkadir et al., 2018). Voluntary retirement is initiated by employees by choice. Compulsory and mandatory forms of retirement are similar but distinct; compulsory retirement is an involuntary retirement dictated by employers, while mandatory retirement occurs when employees reach a predetermined age or benchmark (Abdulkadir et al., 2018). Most individuals who retire do so voluntarily, which is fortunate because voluntary retirement is significantly associated with positive retirement outcomes (Landon & Ritz, 2016; Rhee et al., 2016). A quantitative multiwave study recently conducted by Rhee et al. (2016) confirmed the notion that voluntary retirement is associated with positive retirement experiences. They conducted an analysis of surveys collected from 1,195 adults ages 50 and older and revealed that involuntary retirement was directly negatively associated with health and indirectly negatively associated with mental well-being, while voluntary retirement had an indirect positive association with both health and mental well-being; all of the aforementioned relationships were also found to be mediated by financial control. Cameron and Griffiths (2016) also confirmed the influence of retirement context and type on retirement outcomes among police officers. Among the nine former officers who participated, officers who experienced mandatory or compulsory retirement were more likely to experience negative retirement outcomes, such as depression and feelings of isolation or abandonment.

Mandatory retirement is controversial in some academic and professional circles, primarily due to the perceived injustice of the use of age as a determinant of when someone's career should end (Beck & Williams, 2015). Mandatory retirement is banned in the United States, excluding certain sectors where public safety is a concern (Beck & Williams, 2015). Despite the practice being barred or regulated in many industrialized countries, some research indicates that many individuals who have undergone mandatory retirement would not have continued working much longer if given the option; thus, the degree of impact these laws and regulations have on participation in the labor force remains unclear (Oude-Mulders, 2019). Proponents of mandatory retirement, compulsory retirement, and age-based guidelines/expectations for retirement cite benefits to both workers and businesses in some sectors. Namely, researchers such as Syse et al. (2015) found positive associations between health status and retirement, mental health and retirement, and physical activity/weight loss and retirement among older adults. Syse et al. (2015) studied participants ($N =$

546) were between the ages of 57 and 66 years, a range similar to those used by other researchers who have studied retirement. Due to the variance in the age ranges used to classify average retirement age or age of retirement, however, it remains unclear whether the unique benefits and challenges associated with retirement are more or less prevalent depending on age.

While many researchers have found positive outcomes from the retirement transition, challenges and obstacles have also been found in numerous studies (Henning et al., 2016; Syse et al., 2015). Because the transition to retirement is influenced by several factors, some individuals are more likely to transition and adjust more favorably than others (Henning et al., 2016; Syse et al., 2015; van den Bogaard et al., 2016). Generally speaking, many complications and obstacles associated with retirement can be negated or moderated through careful preretirement planning and preparation (Eagers et al., 2018; van den Bogaard et al., 2016). Individuals who have the opportunity to develop and plan for their own desired trajectory to retirement generally experience more favorable outcomes. Conversely, individuals who must retire involuntarily or without much warning for various reasons are more likely to encounter challenges and experience difficulty during the transition (van den Bogaard et al., 2016)

The immediate period during which individuals transition from a working to retired role can significantly impact retirement outcomes; thus, numerous researchers have studied the nature of this period (Eagers et al., 2018; Syse et al., 2015; Wetzel et al., 2016). A recent systematic literature review conducted by Eagers et al. (2018) revealed that white- and blue-collar workers experienced the retirement transition very differently; the researchers also emphasized the importance of preparation. Eagers et al. concluded by recommending that occupational therapists tailor retirement interventions to the preretirement occupation of their clients. Wetzel et al. (2016) took a different approach to studying the transition to retirement by examining how the adjustment to retirement impacts life satisfaction within the context of the span of an adult life. Score modeling conducted for multiple groups and multiple episodes revealed that the association between life satisfaction and retirement was mediated by education and employment status. While retirement resulted in short-term increased satisfaction among most subjects, long-term satisfaction was experienced by retirees with higher educational attainment, while life satisfaction decreased over time among those with lower educational attainment (Wetzel et al., 2016). Thus, certain forms of social capital and demographic factors can influence how individuals experience retirement and, by association, retirement outcomes.

Many retirees feel a desire to take up new activities or roles to fill their newfound free time and maintain some sense of continuity throughout the transition (Henning et al., 2016). Some take up productive new hobbies, volunteer work, social events, or forms of physical activity. Conversely, the significant change associated with retirement leads other retirees to increase drinking, sedentary behavior, and isolation (Agahi et al., 2018). Working after retirement, primarily on a part-time or volunteer basis, is one strategy that some retirees use to maintain continuity through their transition to retirement and/or to make money. The following subsection includes a discussion of working beyond retirement and how it impacts retirement experiences.

Work After Retirement

A surprising number of retirees return to work in some capacity after transitioning to retirement. Working after retirement decreases the degree of lifestyle change associated with retirement, thus making it a less daunting process to undertake. Part-time work can be used as a gradual transition to leaving one's profession (Dingemans & Henkens, 2017; Dingemans et al., 2017).

The prevalence of bridge employment varies significantly across different regions of the globe. There are many different cultural perspectives and regional norms that influence individuals' decisions to take part in bridge employment. Further, economic conditions in some regions necessitate a greater number of individuals taking part in bridge employment beyond ages typically associated with full retirement (Dingemans et al., 2017).

Changes to policies and laws associated with retirement can significantly impact societal norms and expectations associated with bridge employment and retirement. For instance, disestablishing a default retirement age across the United Kingdom placed significantly more emphasis on employee performance and discretion concerning the appropriate time for employees to retire (Beck & Williams, 2015). To reinforce the benefits and mitigate the drawbacks of prevalent bridge employment, Burkert and Hochfellner (2017) suggested that lawmakers should identify variations between peer groups in the labor market and subsequently align various public policy measures to systematically address each of their concerns and support their transitions to retirement.

The benefits of working after retirement are dependent on certain factors, namely whether individuals are working during retirement due to financial constraints or an inherent desire to continue working (Dingemans & Henkens, 2017; Saraswat, 2017). To test the hypothesis that differences in the life satisfaction experienced by working retirees and full retirees could be explained by income and socioeconomic status, Dingemans and Henkens (2017) analyzed data collected from the Survey of Health, Ageing and Retirement in Europe (N = 53,000). Analysis of the sample of retirees between 60 and 75 years old living in 17 different countries revealed that working retirees, also known as bridge employees, experienced greater life satisfaction and well-being than full retirees. This result was true regardless of whether the researchers controlled for commonly-cited predictors of retirement life satisfaction, including partner status, health, and income (Dingemans & Henkens, 2017). During another recent study of 195 bridge employees, Mazumdar et al. (2017) found that both work performance and well-being outcomes related to "life satisfaction, marital adjustment quality, job satisfaction, commitment, organizational citizenship behavior, co-worker intimacy, and intention to continue working for the employing organization" (p. 105) in retirement were predicted by participants' psychological contract with their employer. Thus, employers can have a significant impact on employees' retirement transitions due to how their professional actions and decisions impact employees' psychological contracts.

Other factors that are associated with participation in bridge employment after retirement include education level, race, marital status, health, job status/title, physical and mental capability, access to work, and pension (Oleksiyenko & Życzyńska-Ciołek, 2018). A recent quantitative analysis of structural determinants of bridge employment participation was conducted by Oleksiyenko and Życzyńska-Ciołek. Analysis of retiree data gathered from the Polish Panel Survey POLPAN revealed educational attainment and degree of professional prestige associated with subjects' preretirement jobs were significant predictors of bridge employment; further, the aforementioned relationship was mediated by subjects' pensions. Another analysis of panel data conducted by Kalenkoski and McCarty (2019) revealed that being older, Black, or having a large amount of nonlabor related income were factors that predicted bridge employment or gradual retirement, while being married, a college graduate, and healthy predicted delaying full retirement. Retirement and bridge employment data collected during another national survey, the National Survey of Health and Development, were also recently analyzed by Stafford et al. (2017). Among older adults up to the age of 68, negative experiences transitioning to retirement and a lesser likelihood of participating in bridge employment were associated with self-reported physical limitations around age 53. Volunteer work and bridge employment were found to be more likely among individuals who performed well on tests of cognition and physical capabilities. Stafford et al. (2017) found these relationships to be consistent regardless of demographic factors including class, occupation, gender, education, and their partner's employment status. The results of these studies highlight the complex interplay of factors that predict bridge employment and the partially conflicting nature of research findings on the topic.

Retiring from Police Work

Participants in this study are retired police officers. While numerous researchers have studied retirement among police officers, many research gaps pertaining to their experiences persist. The nature of retirement among police officers is explored in this section. A subsection details commonly-cited antecedents, determinants, and challenges associated with the retirement of police officers.

The retirement of police officers can differ in many ways in comparison to average retirement experiences across all sectors of the U.S. workforce. Divergence from average retirement experiences is due, primarily, to the nature of retired officers' prior work. Compared to most occupations and job roles, police officers are exposed to a significant number of stressful situations (Leppma et al., 2018; Marchand et al., 2015). Law enforcement officers in many service capacities are routinely exposed to threats, trauma, distrust, danger, violence, and confrontations (Price, 2017). Without the influence of certain protective factors—including coping mechanisms, dissociation, help-seeking behaviors, and social support—many law enforcement employees are susceptible to experiencing occupational difficulties as a result (Marchand et al., 2015). These experiences can stay with officers for years and continue to impact their physical or mental health well into retirement.

The nature of law enforcement places officers at a heightened risk for developing a multitude of physical and psychological health problems, including depression, alcohol abuse, trauma, suicide, and stress-related disorders (Price, 2017; Steinkopf et al., 2015). Some social and health-related issues associated with police work frequently preceed or predict worse issues and further health deterioration. For instance, Violanti et al.(2018) found that domestic abuse and alcohol abuse are common precursors of suicide and self-harm among law enforcement officers. For this reason, researchers and law enforcement leaders have placed a greater emphasis on retirement resources and support for retired officers in recent years (Bracken-Scally et al., 2016; Bullock et al., 2018).

A significant emphasis is placed on the importance of planning in research on retirement; however, researchers such as Washburn (2018) have criticized the lack of resources and planning assistance offered to retired police officers. Namely, Washburn (2018) criticized the disparity between the resources available to officers when they are actively working versus after their retirement:

Police agencies have procedures in play for the mental well-being of officers when it comes to initial hiring and on the job incidents or trauma, but nothing is aligned for those faced to deal with the years following retirement and the emotional distress that may follow. (p. 12)

Further, Washburn (2018) dispelled the notion that the pension received by retired law enforcement officers negated any financial concerns or challenges:

Likewise, even though pensions are set from the start, officers are not equipped to handle financial planning after retirement. The average salary earned after retirement is only a fraction of what they are accustomed to which makes just the basic necessities a struggle for some. As they age, health care costs, along with cost of living expenses will only continue to rise, yet their income will remain the same. Officers need guidance for preparation of this stage and departments should offer financial planning to help them adjust. (p. 13)

The importance of retirement planning and preparation resources for emergency personnel, including police officers, was also emphasized by Bracken-Scally et al. (2016). Six fire and eight ambulance personnel who were interviewed generally indicated that, while they were aware of certain resources that existed to ease their transition to retirement, a lack of awareness and discussion of retirement resources led to additional confusion. Further, the participants noted that the elements of emergency response work that are emotionally and physically stressful are also the elements that make transitioning abruptly to a retired lifestyle more difficult (Bracken-Scally et al., 2016). The sense of purpose, action, and importance associated with emergency response work can be difficult to leave behind. For this reason, many retired emergency workers opt to participate in bridge employment or volunteer work (Dingemans et al., 2017).

While numerous types of emergency responders experience a notable sense of loss when leaving their professional role to retire, there are ultimately other unique and niche retirement concerns that are particularly common in the field of law enforcement (Corpuz, 2020). In a recent phenomenological study, Corpuz (2020) focused on exploring commonalities and differences among participants' lived experiences as former officers and during retirement. Analysis of interview responses from six retired officers yielded the themes of: "(1) satisfaction after retirement; (2) negation of current negative issues in the police service; (3) affliction with the problems in the police service; (4) financial stability and; (5) health problems" (p. 1). Further, there were significantly different responses from officers who retired voluntarily compared to those who retired as the result of a work-related injury. The results both confirmed and disconfirmed previous findings pertaining to the retirement experiences of police officers; notably, the impact of police retirees' health and financial circumstances on retirement outcomes was confirmed.

A multitude of factors influence and shape the retirement experiences of police officers (Bullock et al., 2018). Commonly discussed antecedents, determinants, and challenges associated with the retirement experiences of police officers are discussed below. An emphasis is placed on mental health, social support, and retirement planning in three subsections.

Antecedents, Determinants, and Challenges

Many researchers have sought to conceptualize retirement and how it is experienced by different individuals. Some have developed models or frameworks to describe the complex interplay of retirement factors. Generally speaking, most models account for how external and structural determinants of retirement impact employees differently based on personal or demographic-related factors (Bullock et al., 2019). For instance, mandatory retirement (a structural factor) can influence retirement experiences differently depending on an individual's level of resilience (a personal factor). A review of factors that impact adjustment to retirement was recently conducted by Fadila and Alam (2016) using a cross-sectional descriptive research design. A total of 210 retirees participated by completing self-administered questionnaires. The results of their data analysis revealed that factors which impacted variation in scores on the retirement adjustment scale, retirement resources inventory, and researcher-developed questions were retirees' "gender, marital status, level of education, type of job before retirement, job condition, and place of work," in addition to "adequate resources [such] as physical, financial, social support and mental capacity" (p. 112). Using the results of their research, Fadila and Alam's (2016) provide an overview of the numerous factors and types of factors that have been shown to impact retirement transitions in other studies, which have generally been focused on examining the impact of a smaller number of factors and relationships.

Most researchers have either focused on factors specific to police retirement or general retirement; however, Bullock et al. (2019) recently examined both police-specific and general retirement factors among a sample of retired police officers. Analysis of survey data revealed that gender, having or not having dependent children, rank, the circumstances of retirement, health, degree of preparedness, access to retirement resources, and financial status all significantly impacted retirement experiences. In their study, Bullock et al. support the assertion that retirement resources and programs should be customizable to the extent that employees who are projected to experience specific retirement difficulties are made aware of relevant resources.

For retirees in any line of work, retirement is characterized by a process of significant change (Henning et al., 2016; van den Bogaard et al., 2016). Thus, researchers, including Henning et al. (2016) have emphasized the importance of maintaining continuity as much as possible throughout the transition. Their systematic review of the literature revealed the significance of various adaptive behaviors to ease the transition to retirement. Several studies have confirmed the finding that adaptive behaviors, including bridge employment and adopting new leisure activities, are associated with positive retirement outcomes (Henning et al., 2016). It is important to note that these findings are meant to apply only to the immediate period following retirement that is characterized by a transition away from one's working role and into the role of a retiree.

The nature of the change associated with the transition to retirement is relative (Henning et al., 2016; van den Bogaard et al., 2016). For an individual working a slow-paced, part-time, work-from-home job before retirement, for example, the transition to retirement might seem less jarring or dramatic. Conversely, for someone in a fast-paced and often high-stress job, such as police work, the transition to a more leisurely and unstructured lifestyle of retirement might feel more disorienting (van den Bogaard et al., 2016). While the retiree in the latter example would likely feel a more significant change when transitioning to retirement, some research findings indicate they would also be more likely to experience improved health or retirement outcomes. Analysis of Dutch panel data conducted by van den Bogaard et al. (2016) revealed that among 819 retired individuals and 636 working individuals representing the same age range, those who retired were healthier than those who did not. Further, those who previously held high-stress jobs experienced the most significant self-rated improvements to health following their retirement.

Indeed, numerous researchers have found that the context and circumstances of retirement significantly impact outcomes (Cameron & Griffiths, 2016; Landon & Ritz, 2016; van den Bogaard et al., 2016). This includes factors that are, to a certain extent, within the control of retirees, as well as those that are not. Beyond tangible factors and degrees of preparedness for retirement, even retirees' perceptions of their retirement circumstances can influence outcomes. Landon and Ritz (2016) highlighted a connection in extant literature between factors that impact both individuals' decisions to retire and their contentment once they do retire. This factor has been called the happiness factor by retirement researchers. The happiness factor is identified as a combination of "(a) the sense of control an individual has, (b) their social relationships, and (c) their financial status" (Landon & Ritz, 2016, p. 12). The happiness factor described by researchers including Landon and Ritz can be considered another framework or model of factors that influence the quality of life during retirement.

There is some evidence that indicates that the less retirees are able to control and prepare for the retirement process, the less likely they are to experience favorable retirement outcomes; this explains, in part, why involuntary retirement can be particularly consequential (Cameron & Griffiths, 2016). Qualitative interviews with nine retirees who previously served as chief superintendents or superintendents in the English police force informed Cameron and Griffiths' (2016) research on how involuntary retirement impacts former officers. Both positive and negative outcomes were reported. Positive outcomes included "having increased time for fitness and leisure activities, and entering new careers," while negative outcomes included "inadequate time to prepare for retirement, financial challenges, difficulties navigating the civilian job market, low mood, and feelings of isolation and abandonment" (p. 7). Most researchers have reported generally positive experiences on general retirement and retirement among police officers. Thus, it is notable that among the sample of officers studied by Cameron and Griffiths (2016), all of whom retired involuntarily, more negative outcomes were reported than positive. Another study of retirees who retired involuntarily was recently conducted by Rhee et al. (2016). Using a regression and mediation analysis of data ($n = 1,195$) gathered from the Health and Retirement Study, the researchers revealed negative associations between involuntary retirement and mental health, as well as self-rated health. Conversely, positive relationships were found between voluntary retirement and mental health and voluntary retirement and self-rated health. Financial control was found to mediate all the aforementioned relationships.

Some factors are associated with vulnerabilities or complications during retirement. Shin et al. (2018) used regression and latent class analysis to study retirement vulnerabilities among a sample of 2,617 retirees included in the national U.S. Health and Retirement Study who were above the age of 64. Among those included in the sample, the vulnerability patterns of "Physical and psychological vulnerable (13%), Social vulnerable (35%), Low vulnerable (37%) and Material vulnerable (15%)" emerged (Shin et al., 2018, p. 1006). These themes describe physical and psychological health issues, lack of social support, being at a low risk of experiencing issues during retirement, and lack of resources/capital, respectively. Further, excluding subjects included in the "low vulnerable" subgroup (37%), all others who were vulnerable for one or more reasons had significantly lower well-being during retirement. These results were true regardless of whether controls were in place for education, gender, retirement type (i.e., voluntary/involuntary), and/or age.

Most researchers agree that retirement is a complex and multi-faceted process. It should also be noted that some factors may impact retirement experiences on their own in addition to mediating or mitigating the impact of other factors on retirement (Landon & Ritz, 2016; Rhee et al., 2016). Certain influential factors have been discussed more frequently in association with the retirement outcomes of police officers than others. The proceeding subsections include discussion of the roles of mental health, social support, and financial planning. While these factors may be particularly influential among retired law enforcement officers, numerous other factors also impact or are impacted by retirement outcomes.

Mental Health

Mental health is a research topic that is commonly discussed within the context of retirement and retirement-age samples. Mental health prior to the retirement transition can impact the trajectory of the process; the transition, then, can impact mental health as well. Many retirees generally experience positive emotions and well-being during retirement, often having better self-reported mental health perceptions compared to individuals who are still in the workforce (Syse et al., 2015). Despite this, the psychological experiences of some retirees can also be replete with negative emotions. Denial, stress, anger, and anxiety are some of the common psychological experiences of retirees during their retirement (Abdulkadir et al., 2018). While experiencing negative emotions at different stages of the transition is typical given the degree of change associated with retirement, certain mental health conditions or problems may emerge or be exacerbated by the change (Topa & Valero, 2017).

Depression is a common psychological difficulty among retirees (Shiba et al., 2017; Topa & Valero, 2017). Researchers, including Shiba et al. (2017), have found that retirees in some fields exhibit higher levels of depressive symptoms compared to individuals who are still in the workforce. The threat of loss of resources serves as a factor that contributes to depressive symptoms among retirees (Topa & Valero, 2017). Among retired police officers, the risk of depression is even higher. Out of a sample of 972 retired police officers in Ireland, Black et al. (2013) found that 50% experienced some type or degree of depression. Despite this, the researchers noted that the establishment of enhanced clinical services for retired officers was contributing to a reduction in depression among them at the time of the study. Further, depression frequently exists alongside other comorbid mental health conditions among retired police officers; among a sample of 243 current and former police officers who had been diagnosed with posttraumatic stress disorder (PTSD), Bowler et al. (2016) found that 24.7% also had depression and 47.7% had comorbid anxiety and depression.

Stress and anxiety are also common psychological experiences among retirees during retirement (Saraswat, 2017). Anxiety and stress during retirement are primarily a result of a perceived loss of control in some manner, be it financial or the loss of one's preretirement role (Burkert & Hochfellner, 2017). Resistance to change also frequently accounts for stress and anxiety encountered by police officers during retirement (Steinkopf et al., 2015).

Among police officers specifically, bridge employment is associated with significantly decreased risks for certain mental health conditions, including anxiety, because the degree of change associated with retirement can be lessened (Reisi et al., 2017). Bridge employment can be particularly helpful for mitigating stress and anxiety among retirees who were high-ranking and feel a significant sense of loss towards their prior role (Reisi et al., 2017).

Among police officers in particular, untreated or unaddressed mental health challenges that resulted from work-related incidents before retirement may become apparent once the transition to retirement occurs. While mental health resources and support are always offered to working law enforcement officers, access to these resources becomes more difficult during retirement (Hope, 2017). Further, many departments are characterized by a stigma surrounding discussing or reporting mental health challenges. Law enforcement is a field characterized by perceptions of strength and stability. When working, many officers feel pressured to downplay negative mental health symptoms to avoid being required to take time off. This pressure can be compounded when superior officers are not well trained in identifying officers who need help or may be at risk of serious mental health consequences. Once retired, the stigma and habit of downplaying negative mental health symptoms can persist and lead to conditions remaining untreated (Hope, 2017).

One mental health condition that is disproportionately prevalent among current and former police officers is PTSD (Marchand et al., 2015). Exposure to one or more traumatic events while working can lead to the development of the condition, particularly if proper mental health resources and support are not utilized in the wake of a traumatic event. Particularly severe PTSD can lead to early retirement before officers have time to properly plan and prepare (Yu et al., 2016). Among first responders who were working during the 9/11 terrorist attacks, Yu et al. (2016) found that a PTSD diagnosis increased the likelihood of job loss or early retirement, particularly when one or more comorbid conditions were also present. Coping strategies and certain demographic factors may have a protective effect in terms of moderating the development of PTSD among retired law enforcement officers (Nho & Kim, 2017). Nho and Kim's (2017) cross-sectional analysis of 226 retired crime scene investigators from metropolitan police departments revealed that high levels of resilience and social support were associated with a lower risk of developing PTSD. Comorbid conditions can impact the effectiveness of certain coping strategies and approaches. In addition to social support, Leppma et al. (2018) found that satisfaction with life and gratitude also had a protective effect, whereby police officers were more likely to experience posttraumatic growth (PTG) than posttraumatic stress in the wake of traumatic events.

Suicide is also particularly prevalent among current and former police officers; in many cases, suicide results from one or more mental health conditions remaining untreated (Violanti et al., 2018). Many retired law enforcement officers carry over stressors and traumatic experiences from their careers into retirement that impact their likelihood of suicide. A study of the stressors associated with suicide among current and former law enforcement officers was recently conducted by Violanti et al. (2018). Use of the PRISMA methodology of systematically reviewing literature revealed a significant positive association between the stressors of "lack of organizational support, traumatic events, shift work, stigma associated with asking for help, or problems associated with fitting in with the police culture" (Violanti et al., 2018, p. 4) and suicide among current and former officers. Domestic violence and alcohol use were also shown to be significantly associated with suicidal ideation (Violanti et al., 2018).

Some research evidence indicates promising improvements in mental health resources and outcomes among current and former police officers; in particular, the stigma surrounding help-seeking behaviors and mental health treatment has begun to decline in recent years (Price, 2017). Increased research focus on retired police officers has brought increased awareness to the importance of cohesive efforts between police departments and officers to ensure a successful retirement transition. Recently, innovative programs such as the Peers as Law Enforcement Support (PALS) program have been implemented in the United States to help law enforcement officers adequately and comfortably address personal concerns and challenges so that they do not persist through an officer's career and into retirement (Hasselt et al., 2019).

In other ways, however, conditions seem to be worsening. Law enforcement leaders have witnessed an increase in applications for disability retirement pensions based on physical and psychiatric medical diagnoses (Price, 2017). Psychiatric sequelae associated with police work, namely "trauma-related symptoms, depression, alcohol-use disorders, and stress-related medical conditions" (Price, 2017, p. 114) are leading otherwise fit and capable officers to retire early, in many cases before they would prefer to retire. Thus, there is still a significant amount of work to be done before mental health conditions and symptoms become a less common negative influence on police officers' retirement experiences.

Social Support

Social support and relationships also play an important role in the successful transition of many retirees (Haslam et al., 2018). Social support can include individual friendships and relationships in addition to relationships with communities and within organizations. Research on retirement has shown that increased social interaction can facilitate better retirement experiences and more positive mental health outcomes (Haslam et al., 2018; Leppma et al., 2018; Shiba et al., 2017; Shin et al., 2018). Further, social support can moderate negative experiences and concerns associated with retirement, including posttraumatic stress, stressful events, financial concerns, and a sense of loss after leaving one's working role (Leppma et al., 2018).

Numerous researchers have found significant associations between positive retirement outcomes and social support. Social support was found to be a protective factor that decreased the likelihood of food insecurity among retired Americans (n = 1,164) in a study conducted by Wang and Bishop (2019). In their study, Karlin et al. (2019) revealed, through interviews with 60 retirees, that social support significantly impacted factors such as health satisfaction and quality of life during retirement. Gendered differences were found pertaining to retirement resources, making social support more crucial among female retirees.

The type of social support that is available to retirees may also significantly impact how retirees adjust to retirement, according to Lam et al. (2018). The researchers gathered data about the retirement experiences of 10,513 retirees who resided in 51 different countries from the World Values Survey. The analysis revealed that the well-being and health of retirees were significantly and positively predicted by inclusion in multiple social groups. Further, this association was stronger in countries that are characterized by individualism over collectivism. Due to the findings of their study, Lam et al. (2018) suggest that it is not only the availability of social support that impacts retirement outcomes, but also the number of sources of support one has or the size of their social network. Particularly in individualistic countries such as the United States, retirees may benefit from seeking multiple sources of social support, including support groups, friends, neighbors, and clubs.

Many retirees perceive a sense of social isolation once retired (Burkert & Hochfellner, 2017). Social support and interaction with other people can act as a buffer for negative affect among retired individuals. Thus, without sufficient social support, many retirees are prone to being overwhelmed with negative feelings or emotions (Shin et al., 2018).

Perceived isolation is coupled with the loss of the sense of community or comradery associated with one's department among retired police officers (Hope, 2017). Hence, many retirees engage in bridge employment or join new organizations after retiring (Dingemans et al., 2017). This behavior is not necessarily motivated by the increased need for financial income but the continued need for social interaction and support (Dingemans et al., 2017). New group membership is one way retired police officers may socially adjust to the loss of their professional and social identity. A recent multiwave study conducted by Haslam et al. (2018) revealed significant associations between life satisfaction and new group membership among samples of 302 and 121 retirees, respectively. The results indicated that membership and identification with new groups following retirement decrease the sense of loss and change associated with the transition, making retirees feel more secure about not being known for their work or professional capacity.

Some researchers have even suggested that other negative outcomes and consequences associated with retirement can be mitigated if an individual's social support system is strong enough (Shiba et al., 2017; Umukoro & Adejuwon, 2017). Associations between geriatric depression and retirement status within a sample of 62,438 Japanese adults above the age of 64 was recently studied by Shiba et al. (2017). Using regression analysis, the authors revealed that while depression symptoms significantly increased among many participants after they retired (33% of men and 29% of women), those who reported continued social and recreational participation following retirement were significantly less likely to report depression symptoms. The association between depression symptoms and social participation was shown to be particularly strong among individuals in lower-class, or blue-collar, occupations (Shiba et al., 2017). Umukoro and Adejuwon (2017) conducted a similar study, which looked at the mediation of certain psychological retirement antecedents among 230 retired police officers working in Nigeria. Using regression analysis, the authors revealed that significant predictors of retirement satisfaction were health quality, career success, and leisure satisfaction. Associations between health quality and retirement satisfaction, as well as career success and retirement satisfaction, were found to be partially mediated by social support, while the association between leisure satisfaction and retirement was fully mediated by social support (Umukoro & Adejuwon, 2017). The results of these studies demonstrate how social support may have a more significant role in terms of predicting retirement outcomes than other commonly-cited factors, including former occupation or mental health symptoms.

Social support is particularly influential among current and retired police officers for multiple reasons (Kirschman, 2018). Namely, the support of friends and family is particularly influential because police officers are less likely than individuals in other professions to disclose mental health problems or adverse experiences to clinical professionals. Many retired police officers feel significantly more comfortable discussing feelings and experiences with others who have served in a law enforcement capacity because they feel less stigmatized and more likely to be understood. It is, however, important to note that effective social support is not an adequate replacement for clinically addressing or treating diagnosed mental illnesses among police officers (Kirschman, 2018). Ultimately, a multifaceted approach is necessary to properly address mental health symptoms when they become disruptive to a retiree's quality of life and well-being.

Preparation and Financial Planning

Retirement preparation is one of the most important factors that can be critical to the successful transition of individuals to retirement (Burkert & Hochfellner, 2017; Rhee et al., 2016; Topa et al., 2018). Financial planning should be a single, but substantial, component of a multifaceted approach to retirement preparation (Spraggins, 2019); however, much extant literature on the topic of retirement preparation centers solely on financial planning and/or means of easing the financial transition from actively working to retirement, such as bridge employment.

The retirement of police officers often involves the provision of a pension to supplement typical social security benefits. The pension and benefits afforded to police officers varies considerably across different states and circumstances of retirement (see Table 1). Officers must reach a certain age and/or serve for a certain length of time before they are eligible for their pension. In some states, partial benefits can be collected before officers reach these thresholds, while in others, not reaching these thresholds means forfeiting the pension.

Table 1.

State Governments' Public Safety Retirement Plans

STATE AND PLAN	EMPLOYEES COVERED	AGE AND SERVICE REQUIREMENTS FOR NORMAL RETIREMENT	REQUIREMENTS FOR EARLY RETIREMENT WITH REDUCED BENEFITS	BENEFIT FORMULA FOR NORMAL SERVICE RETIREMENT AND SOCIAL SECURITY COVERAGE	COMPUTATION OF FINAL AVERAGE SALARY (FAS)	EMPLOYEE CONTRIBUTION
Alabama Employees' Retirement System As of 1/1/13	State and local police and firefighter members	56/10 Vesting: 10 years	N/A	1.65% times FAS times years of service Social Security Coverage: Yes	Average of 5 highest years of the last 10	7%
Alabama Employees' Retirement System As of 1/1/13	State police (includes investigators)	56/10 Vesting: 10 years	N/A	2.375% times FAS times years of service Social Security Coverage: No	Average of 5 highest years of the last 10	10%
Alaska Public Employees' Retirement System: Defined Benefit Plan	Peace officers and firefighters statewide who entered service before July 1, 2006	20 years of contributory service in the plan Vesting: 5 years	Age 55 for employees entering the plan on or after July 1, 1996	2% times first 10 years times FAS; plus 2.5% times all years after 10 times FAS Social Security Coverage: No	Average of 3 highest consecutive years	7.5%
Alaska Public Employees' Retirement System: Defined Contribution Plan	Peace officers and firefighters statewide who entered service on or after July 1, 2006	Any/25 Vesting: 100% at 5 years; 75% at 4 years; 50% at 3 years; 25% at 2 years	N/A	Not applicable. Benefit is based on the value of the member's account. Social Security Coverage: No	N/A	8%
Arizona Correction Officers' Retirement Plan as of 1/1/12	Designated employees in the state departments of corrections and juvenile justice and certain dispatchers and detention and probation officers	62/10; 52.5/25 Vesting: 5 years	N/A	62.5% of member's FAS plus 2.5% of FAS for each year of credited service over 25, including fractional years. Members who are 52.5 with 25 years of service but not 25 years of credited service: 2.5% times FAS times years of credited service Social Security Coverage: Yes	Average of 60 highest consecutive months in the last 10 years	Non-dispatchers: 8.41%; Dispatchers: 7.96%, or 50% of the member's total contribution from the previous fiscal year and the combined employer contribution rate, whichever is lower. The employee contribution rate shall not be less than 7.65% of the member's salary.
Arizona Public Safety Personnel Retirement System as of 1/1/2012	Certified state and local police officers and firefighters	52.5/25; Any/25 Vesting: 5 years	Age 52.5 Benefit reduction of 4% for each year the member is short 25 years of service.	62.5% of the average monthly benefit compensation for the first 25 years of credited service plus 2.5% of the average monthly benefit compensation for each year over 25 years of credited service to a maximum of 80% of FAS Social Security Coverage: Varies by local government	Average of 60 highest consecutive months in the last 20 years of credited service	8.65% after June 30, 2011
Arkansas Local Police and Fire Retirement System	Employees of political subdivisions of the state	Any/28; 55/20; 60/5 Vesting: 5 years	Any/25 years of earned credit; 50/20 Benefit reduction of ½ of 1% of benefit for each month applicant is below age 55	Service not covered by Social Security: 2.94% times FAS times years of service; Service covered by Social Security: Until reaching the age of unreduced Social Security benefits—2.94% times FAS times years of service, thereafter—1.94% times FAS times years of service; Local employers may provide enhanced benefits. Social Security Coverage: Varies by local government	Average of 36 highest consecutive months in the last 10 years	Covered by Social Security: 2.5% Not covered by Social Security: 8.5%
Arkansas State Police Retirement System: Tier 2	State police	65/5; 30 years of service Vesting: 5 years	With 20 years of service if within 5 years of normal retirement age (65)	1.55% times FAS times years of service, plus a temporary benefit of 0.513% times FAS time years of service for those who retire before the age of 62 until they reach that age. Social Security Coverage: Yes	Average of 4 highest years, including partial years	Noncontributory
California Public Employee Retirement System	Local Safety Members: law enforcement, fire suppression, other public safety	50/5 Vesting: 5 years (10 years for Tier II members)	N/A	Various formulas apply depending on category of employee and on employer's choice of plan. Ranges in broad summary are 2% or 2.5% at age 50 or 3% at 50 or 3% at 55. Benefits are capped, variously, at 80% or 90% of final salary. Social Security Coverage: Varies by local government	Average of 12 highest months or 36 highest months, depending upon employer choice of plan	For FY 2011: 8% to 13% depending on type of plan and whether employees are covered by Social Security
California Public Employee Retirement System	State Highway Patrol Safety Members from Department of Forestry, Highway Patrol, Youth Authority, and Department of Corrections	50/5 Vesting: 5 years (10 years for Tier II members)	N/A	Various formulas apply to various categories of employees, generally in the range of 2% or 2.5% at age 50 to 3% at 50 or 3% at 55. Benefits are capped, variously, at 80% or 90% of final salary. Social Security Coverage: Varies by local government	Depending on classification of employee, average of 12 highest months or 36 highest months	For FY 2011: 9% to 11% depending on plan type and whether employees are covered by Social Security. Highway Patrol: 10%
Colorado Fire and Police Pension Association: Standard Defined Benefit Plan	Statewide plan for police and firefighters; employers choose to affiliate	55/25 Vesting: 5 years	30 years of service credit; Age 50 Benefit reduction will apply.	2% times FAS for first 10 years of service credit plus 2.5% times FAS for ensuing years of service credit Social Security Coverage: Varies by local government	Average of 3 highest years	Standard Defined Benefit Plan: 8%
Colorado Public Employee Retirement Association	State trooper and Bureau of Investigation provisions	Any/50; 50/75; 55/20; 65/5 Vesting: 5 years	50/20; 60/5 Benefit reduction will apply.	For normal retirement for those becoming eligible to retire after January 1, 2011, 2.5% times FAS times years of service Social Security Coverage: No	Average of 3 highest 12-month periods of service – not necessarily consecutive nor necessarily the last 36 months of employment	12.5% through June 30, 2012; 10.0% thereafter

System	Covered Members	Normal Retirement / Vesting	Early Retirement / Benefit Reduction	Benefit Formula / Social Security Coverage	Final Average Salary (FAS)	Employee Contribution
Indiana 1977 Police Officers' and Firefighters' Pension and Disability Fund	Local governments' police and firefighters, park rangers and certain other law enforcement personnel	52/20 Vesting: 20 years	50 Benefit reduction will apply.	Benefit is 50% of the salary of a first-class officer (as determined by the city in which the applicant was employed) at the time of retirement, plus an additional benefit of 1% for each 6 months of service over 20 years, to a maximum benefit of 74%. Social Security Coverage: No in most cases—varies by local government.	N/A	6% of the salary of a first-class officer (as determined by the city employing the member) Members with more than 32 years of service are not required to contribute.
Iowa Municipal Fire and Police Retirement System	Local governments' police and firefighters	55/22 Vesting: 4 years if termination before age 55 or at least 4 years but less than 22 years after age 55	N/A	66% of FAS, plus 2% additional benefit for each year of service in excess of 22, with the benefit capped at 82% of FAS Social Security Coverage: No	Average of 36 highest months	9.4%
Iowa Peace Officers' Retirement System	State Patrol, Capitol Police, state investigative force and State Fire Marshal	55/22 Vesting: 4 years	50 Benefit reduction will apply.	60.5% of FAS, plus 2.75% for each years in excess of 22 years, to a maximum benefit of 88% of FAS Social Security Coverage: No	Average of 36 highest months	9.35% May be increased by administrative action to a maximum of 11.5% if certain conditions apply.
Iowa Public Employees' Retirement System	Protection occupations: correctional officers, emergency medical technicians, conservation officers, fire and police in smaller cities	55 Vesting: 4 years or age 55	N/A	Approximately 2.73% of FAS for each year of service through 22 years plus 1.5% of FAS for each subsequent year of service through 30; Benefits are capped at 72% of FAS Social Security Coverage: Yes	Average of 3 highest calendar years, with anti-spiking controls	For FY 2012: 6.65% For FY 2013: 6.84%
Iowa Public Employees' Retirement System	Sheriffs and deputies	55; 50/22 if member is a sheriff or deputy at time of retirement. Vesting: 4 years or age 55	N/A	2.73% of FAS for each year of service through 22 years plus 1.5% of FAS for each subsequent year of service through 30; Benefits are capped at 72% of FAS.	Average of 3 highest calendar years, with anti-spiking controls	For FY 2012: 9.83% For FY 2013: 9.90%
Connecticut Hazardous Duty Plan Tier IIA	Hazardous Duty: various state and local police, fire, other public safety, protective services and institutional personnel	Any/20 Vesting: 5 years	55/10 years of vested service	50% of final average salary for first 20 years, plus 2% of FAS for each additional year Social Security Coverage: Yes	Average of 3 highest years	5%
Delaware County and Municipal Police and Firefighters Pension Plan	Various local government fire and public safety members	62/10; 20 years of credited service ; Rule of 75 Vesting: 5 years	N/A	2.5% times FAS times years of service for the first 20 years of service, plus 3.5% times FAS multiplied for any additional years of service Social Security Coverage: Varies by local government	Average of 36 highest months	7%
Delaware New State Police Plan	State police officers	62/10; 20 years of credited service ; Rule of 75 Vesting: 10 years	N/A	Sum of 2.5% times FAS multiplied by up to 20 years of credited service under the New State Police Plan, plus 3.5% of FAS multiplied by all years of service exceeding 20 under the New State Police Plan Social Security Coverage: No	Average of 36 highest months	7%
Florida Retirement System Special Risk Class as of July 1, 711	Various state and local police, fire, other public safety, protective services and institutional personnel	Age 60 and vested (8 years); 25 years of creditable service; Age 57 with 30 years of creditable and military service; 33 years of creditable service Vesting: 8 years	At any age: benefit is reduced by 5% for each year the applicant is short of normal retirement age (60).	3% times FAS times years of service. Benefit factor for certain purchased service is 2% Social Security Coverage: Yes	Average of 8 highest fiscal years	3%
Georgia Employees' Retirement System State Employees' Pension and Savings Plan, a hybrid plan; the DB component is described here	State Corrections Probation officers; Natural Resources Conservation Officers; Bureau of Investigation Officers; State Patrol; State Revenue Agents and Investigators; State Patrol and Public Safety	55/10; 30 years of service Vesting: 10 years	25 years of creditable service Benefit reduction will apply.	1% times FAS times years of service. Employees may also contribute to the 401(k) component of the hybrid, earning a partial employer match for contributions up to 3% of salary. Employees may opt out of the 401(k) component if they choose. Social Security Coverage: Yes	Average of 24 highest months	FY 2012: 1.25%
Hawaii Employees' Retirement System New members as of 7/1/12	State and local police officers, firefighters, and a wide range of other public safety personnel	55/25; 60/10 Vesting: 10 years	N/A	Multiplier reduced to 2.25% and vesting extended from 5 years to 10 Social Security Coverage: No	Average of 5 highest 12-month periods	14.2%
Idaho Public Employees' Retirement System	Police officers and firefighters	60/5; Rule of 80 between ages 60 and 65 for members with mixed fire/police and general service credit. Vesting: 5 years	Age 50; Ages 50-55 for those with mixed service. Benefit reduction factors apply.	2.3% times FAS times years of service Social Security Coverage: Yes	Average of 42 highest consecutive months	7.69%
Illinois State Employees' Retirement System: Alternative Formula, Tier 2	State police, firefighters and corrections officers	60/20 Vesting: 10 years	N/A	Not covered by Social Security: 3% times FAS times years of service Covered by Social Security: 2.5% times FAS times years of service Social Security Coverage: Varies by local government	Average of highest 96 months of last 108, with FAS capped at $106,800, which is annually adjusted for inflation	Covered by Social Security: 8.5%; Not covered by Social Security: 12.5%; Contribution base capped at $106,800 for FY2012, cap annually adjusted
Indiana State Police Benefit System: 1987 Plan	State police officers	25 years of service, no later than age 55 Vesting: 5 years	50 with benefit reduction for less than 25 years of service	For 25 years of service: 50% of FAS, plus accrual rates of 5% to 8% for additional years to a total of 32 years or a maximum of 70% of FAS Social Security Coverage: No	Average of highest 36 consecutive months	6% of salary

Indiana 1977 Police Officers' and Firefighters' Pension and Disability Fund	Local governments' police and firefighters, park rangers and certain other law enforcement personnel	52/20 Vesting: 20 years	50 Benefit reduction will apply.	Benefit is 50% of the salary of a first-class officer (so determined by the city in which the applicant was employed) at the time of retirement, plus an additional benefit of 1% for each 6 months of service over 20 years, to a maximum benefit of 74%. Social Security Coverage: No in most cases—varies by local government.	N/A	6% of the salary of a first-class officer (as determined by the city employing the member) Members with more than 32 years of service are not required to contribute.
Iowa Municipal Fire and Police Retirement System	Local governments' police and firefighters	55/22 Vesting: 4 years if termination before age 55 or at least 4 years but less than 22 years after age 55	N/A	66% of FAS, plus 2% additional benefit for each year of service in excess of 22, with the benefit capped at 82% of FAS Social Security Coverage: No	Average of 36 highest months	9.4%
Iowa Peace Officers' Retirement System	State Patrol, Capitol Police, state investigative force and State Fire Marshal	55/22 Vesting: 4 years	50 Benefit reduction will apply.	60.5% of FAS, plus 2.75% for each years in excess of 22 years, to a maximum benefit of 88% of FAS Social Security Coverage: No	Average of 36 highest months	9.35% May be increased by administrative action to a maximum of 11.3% if certain conditions apply.
Iowa Public Employee Retirement System	Protection occupations: correctional officers, emergency medical technicians, conservation officers, fire and police in smaller cities	55 Vesting: 4 years or age 55	N/A	Approximately 2.73% of FAS for each year of service through 22 years plus 1.5% of FAS for each subsequent year of service through 30; Benefits are capped at 72% of FAS Social Security Coverage: Yes	Average of 3 highest calendar years, with anti-spiking controls	For FY 2012: 6.65% For FY 2013: 6.84%
Iowa Public Employees' Retirement System	Sheriffs and deputies	55; 50/22 if member is a sheriff or deputy at time of retirement. Vesting: 4 years or age 55	N/A	2.73% of FAS for each year of service through 22 years plus 1.5% of FAS for each subsequent year of service through 30; Benefits are capped at 72% of FAS. Social Security Coverage: Yes	Average of 5 highest calendar years, with anti-spiking controls	For FY 2012: 9.83% For FY 2013: 9.96%
Kansas Police and Firemen's Retirement System Tier II members	Highway patrol, bureau of investigation, regents, county and municipal public safety personnel and EMT	50/25; 55/20; 60/15 Vesting: 15 years (Tier II members)	Age 50 with 20 years of service Benefit reduction will apply.	2.5% times FAS times years of service, capped at 32 Social Security Coverage: No	Average of 3 highest of last 5 years	7%; 5% after 32 years of membership
Kentucky Retirement System	State police and state or county employees with hazardous duty	20 years of service; 55 with 5 years hazardous duty service Vesting: 5 years if under age 65; 4 years if over 65	Age 55 with less than 5 years hazardous duty service; 50 with 15 years of hazardous duty service Benefit reduction will apply.	2.5% times FAS times years of service for state police and county hazardous employees; 2.49% for state employees with hazardous duties Social Security Coverage: Yes	Average of 3 highest fiscal year' salaries; must include at least 24 months of service; need not be consecutive	8%
Louisiana Firefighters' Retirement System as of 1/1/12	Municipal firefighters	62/12; 60/20; 55/30 Vesting: 12 years	60/10 Benefit reduction will apply.	3.5% times FAS times years of service, total benefit cannot exceed 100% of FAS Social Security Coverage: No	Average of highest 60 months	8%
Louisiana State Police Retirement System	Police employed after 9/8/78	50/10; 25 years of service Vesting: 25 years	N/A	3.33% times FAS times years of service Social Security Coverage: No	Average of highest 36 months	8.5%
Louisiana Sheriffs' Pension and Relief Fund, as of 1/1/12	Sheriffs, deputies, and sheriffs' non-deputied employees with salaries above $800 per month	62/12; 60/20; 55/30 Vesting: 12 years	Reduced retirement available at 60/10 with actuarial and early retirement (ages 50-55) available only to members of earlier tiers	3% times FAS times years of service; Benefit cannot exceed 100% of FAS. Social Security Coverage: No	Average of 60 highest months	9.8% to 10.25% as determined by the Board of Trustees
Maine Public Employees' Retirement System: Participating Local Districts Plans	Local government employees other than teachers	There are numerous plans with substantial variations, available to local governments' public safety employees at the discretion of the local government. See note. Social security coverage: No			Average of 3 highest years	3% to 8%; 8.65% for the first 25 years of service in the plan; 7.65% thereafter
Maine Public Employees' Retirement System	State police and investigators hired on or after 9/18/84	25 years of service Vesting: 5 years or 1 year if at retirement age	N/A	50% of AFC for 25 years under the plan and 2% of AFC for each additional year Social Security Coverage: No	Average of 3 highest years	8.65% for the first 25 years of service in the plan; 7.65% thereafter
Maine Public Employees' Retirement System	Inland Fisheries and Wildlife Wardens and Marine Resources Wardens	25 years of service Vesting: 5 years or 1 year if at retirement age	N/A	50% of AFC for 25 years under the plan and 2% of AFC for each additional year Social Security Coverage: No	Average of 3 highest years	8.65% for the first 25 years of service in the plan; 7.65% thereafter
Maryland State Retirement and Pension System: Correctional Employees as of 7/1/11	Correctional officers, other security officers, specified other corrections employees	55/5 for most members; 60/5 for certain institutional employees; 20 years of service, five of which must be in covered employment Vesting: 10 years	Available for those entering the Plan on or after June 30, 2006; At least 10 but less than 20 years of service; Same benefit formula applies	1/55 of the product of FAS and years of service Social Security Coverage: Yes	Average of 5 highest years	5%
Maryland State Retirement and Pension System: Law Enforcement Officers as of 7/1/11	Wide variety of law enforcement and protective occupations, mainly state governments	25 years of service; or age 50 Vesting: 10 years	N/A	2% times FAS times years of service, capped at 60% of FAS Social Security Coverage: Yes	Average of 5 highest years Salary increases of more than 20% are not automatically included in the calculation of FAS, unless due to promotion.	7%
Maryland State Retirement and Pension System: State Police Plan as of 7/1/11	Sworn officers and cadets only	25 years of service; or age 50; Mandatory retirement at 60 Vesting: 10 years	N/A	2.55% times FAS times years of service, with a maximum of 28 years of service credit Social Security Coverage: No	Average of 5 highest years	8%
Massachusetts State Employee Retirement System: Group 3 as of 4/2/12	State Police	55/10; 20 years; Mandatory retirement at 65 unless a member needs to serve longer to meet 20-year requirement Vesting: 10 years	N/A	At 20 years of service, 50% of final year's compensation, plus 2.5% for each additional year of service to a maximum of 75% of final salary Social Security Coverage: No	Final 12 months of classification	12% plus 2% of salary in excess of $30,000 per year

System	Members covered	Normal retirement	Early retirement	Benefit	FAS	Employee contribution
Massachusetts State Employee Retirement System; Group 4 as of 4/2/12	State and local public safety officers, officials, and certain correction officers	50; Vesting: 10 years	N/A	Benefit factors depend upon age at retirement. 2011 legislation provides a benefit factor of 1.45% of FAS at age 50 for each year of service, up to a benefit factor of 2.5% of FAS at 57 or older. Social Security Coverage: No	Average of 5 highest years	9% plus 2% of salary in excess of $30,000 per year
Michigan State Police Retirement System	Enlisted officers but not other employees	Any age, 25 years of service credit; Age 50 with 10 years of service credit; Vesting: 10 years	Deferred benefits available for those who leave service with between 10 and 25 years of service	Regular retirement (after 25 years of service): 60% of FAS. Social Security Coverage No	Average of last 2 years' compensation	Noncontributory
Michigan local governments: See notes	See notes					
Minnesota Public Employee Retirement Association, Police and Fire Fund	Local government police and firefighters and Hennepin County paramedics and EMTs	55/10; 65/1; Vesting: Gradual, ranging from 50% at five years of service to 100% at 10 years of service	50/10; Any/30	3% times FAS times years of police & fire service. Social Security Coverage: Yes	Average of 5 highest years	6.25%
Minnesota State Patrol Plan	State patrol and other state officers who have the power of arrest	55/5; Vesting: 5 years	50/5; Benefit reduction will apply.	3% times FAS times years of service. Social Security Coverage: No	Average of 5 highest years	12.4%
Minnesota State Retirement System Correctional Plan as of 7/1/10	Correctional and other employees responsible for inmate care	Age 55; Vesting: Gradual, ranging from 50% at five years of service to 100% at 10 years of service	Age 50; Benefit reduction will apply.	2.4% times FAS times years of service. Social Security Coverage: Yes	Average of 5 highest years	8.6%
Mississippi Highway Safety Patrol Retirement System	Sworn officers	55/5; Any/25; Vesting: 5 years	45/20, with an actuarial reduction for each year below 25 or age 55, whichever is less	2.5% times FAS times years of service, capped at 100% of FAS. Social Security Coverage: Yes	Average of 4 highest consecutive years	7.25%
Mississippi Public Employee Retirement System Tier 4	All other public safety members	65/8; Any/30; Vesting: 8 years	60/8, with an actuarial reduction for each year below 30 or age 65, whichever is less	2% times FAS times years of service, plus 2.5% times FAS times years of service in excess of 36. Social Security Coverage: Most—varies by local government	Average of 4 highest years	9%
Missouri Department of Transportation and Highway Patrol Employees' Retirement System	Uniformed patrol employees	60/5; Rule of 80 with a minimum age of 48; Vesting: 5 years	57/5; Benefit reduction will apply.	1.7% times FAS times years of service; Supplement of 0.8% of FAS for members who retire under the 80-and-out option until they reach age 62. Social Security Coverage: Yes	Average of 3 highest years	Noncontributory
Missouri Local Government Employees' Retirement System	Police and firefighters	55; Rule of 80 if employer chooses to offer it; Vesting: 5 years	50; Benefit reduction will apply.	The system provides a number of benefit factors among which the employing government may choose. These include programs that provide a temporarily higher benefit until the recipient reaches 65. Social Security Coverage: Optional with employing government	Average of 3 or 5 highest years, as determined by employing government	Member employers choose whether plans will be contributory or noncontributory. Contributory plan member employees pay 4%.
Montana Public Employee Retirement Administration	Firefighters' Unified Retirement System	20 years of service; 50/5; Vesting: 5 years	N/A	2.5% times FAS times years of service. Social Security Coverage: No	Average of 3 highest consecutive years	10.7%
Montana Public Employee Retirement Administration	Game Wardens and Peace Officers' Retirement System	50/20; 55/5; Vesting: 5 years	N/A	2.5% times FAS times years of service. Social Security Coverage: Yes	Average of 5 highest consecutive years	9%
Montana Public Employee Retirement Administration	Highway Patrol Officers' Retirement System	20 years of service; Vesting: 5 years	N/A	2.5% times FAS times years of service. Social Security Coverage: No	Average of 3 highest consecutive years	9.05%
Montana Public Employee Retirement Administration	Municipal Police Officers' Retirement System	20 years of service; 50/5; Vesting: 5 years	N/A	2.5% times FAS times years of service. Social Security Coverage: No	Last consecutive 36 months	9%
Montana Public Employee Retirement Administration	Sheriffs' Retirement System	20 years of service; Vesting: 5 years	50/5; Benefit reduction will apply.	2.5% times FAS times years of service. Social Security Coverage: Yes	Average of 5 highest consecutive years	10.115%

Nebraska Public Employees' Retirement Systems Nebraska State Patrol Retirement Plan	State Patrol: sworn officers only	50/25; Any/30 Vesting: Gradual ranging from 10% at 6 years to 100% at 10 years Mandatory retirement at 60	50/10 Benefit reduction will apply.	3.0% times FAS times years of service; Capped at 75% of FAS Social Security Coverage: No	Average of 3 highest years	19% through June 30, 2013; 16% thereafter
Nevada Public Employees' Retirement System Plan for Police and Fire Members as of 1/1/10	Highway Patrol; local governments' police and firefighters; some game wardens, park rangers and corrections officers, depending on responsibilities	50/20; 60/10; 65/5; Any/30 Vesting: 5 years	Any age with 5 years of service Benefit reduction will apply.	2.5% times FAS times years of service Social Security Coverage: No	Average of 36 highest consecutive months; anti-spiking provisions apply	Employer-paid plan (local government employees and optional for state employees; employer makes entire contribution). 39.75% Employee/employer paid: Contribution is split 50/50 and employee receives a refundable no remission of employment. 20.25% employee share.
New Hampshire Retirement System: Group II as of 7/1/11	State and local police and firefighters, correctional officers, other public safety	Age 60; Latter of age 52.5 or 25 years of service Vesting: 10 years	50/25 Benefit reduction will apply.	2 % times FAS times years of creditable service for those who are not vested on 1/1/12 Social Security Coverage: No	Average of 3 highest years	Police: 11.55% Firefighters: 11.8% Member contributions cease for members vested before January 1, 2012 with creditable service in excess of 40 years. Member contributions cease for all other fire and police members with creditable service in excess of 42.5 years.
New Jersey Police and Firemen's Retirement System Tier III as of 6/28/11	State, county and municipal police and firefighters	Age 55; Mandatory at age 65 Vesting: 10 years	N/A	Less than 20 years of service, 2% of FAS for each year of service; 20 to 25 years, 50% of FAS; At least 25 years of service, 60% of FAS plus 1% per year for additional years, not to exceed 65% of FAS Social Security Coverage: Most: Varies by local government	Average salary upon which pension contributions were based for any three fiscal years that provide the highest average	10%. The contribution rate for Tier II members is applied to the pensionable salary up to a limit based on the annual maximum wage for Social Security deduction: $110,100 in 2012. Tier II members who earn in excess of the annual compensation limit will be enrolled in the Defined Contribution Retirement Program in addition to the PFRS. A contribution of 5.5% of the salary in excess of the limit (plus 3% from the employer) will be deposited in a DCRP account.
New Jersey State Police Retirement System: Tier II (members as of May 21, 2010)	Troopers and officers of the Division of State Police	20 years of service Mandatory at 55 Vesting: 10 years	Deferred retirement is available before 55/10	At 20 to 25 years, 50% of FAS. With 25 years or more of service credit, 65% of FAS plus 1% for each year of creditable service over 25 years but not to exceed 30 years. The maximum benefit is 70% of FAS. Social Security Coverage: No	Average salary upon which pension contributions were based for any three fiscal years that provide the highest average	9%. The provisions described above for NJ Police and Firefighters also apply to state police.
New Mexico Public Employees' Retirement Association	Local governments' police and fire members	Generally, 20 years Vesting: 5 years	N/A	A variety of plans with retirement multipliers ranging from 2% to 3.5% Social Security Coverage: No in most cases—varies by local government	Average of 36 highest months	A variety of plans provide for employee contribution rates that range from 7% to 16.3% for police and fire members
New Mexico Public Employees' Retirement Association: State Police and Adult Correctional Officers Plan 1 as of 7/1/11	State Police and adult correctional officers	25 years of service credit Vesting: 5 years	N/A	3% times FAS times years of service times 1.2, capped at 80% of FAS The '1.2' is a "service enhancement factor." Social Security Coverage: No	Average of 36 highest months	10.35%
New York State and Local Retirement System: State Police Tier 5 effective 1/9/10.	State Police	20 years of service Vesting: 10 years	Before 20 years of service, a lower benefit calculation applies. See the cell to the right. Vesting is at 10 years and members may receive vested benefits at 55/10	With 20 years of State Police service credit, 50% of FAS plus 1.66% of FAS for each year of creditable service in excess of 20 years. For Tier 5, the benefit is capped at 70% of FAS. For those with less than 20 years of service, the benefit equals 2.5% of FAS for each year of creditable service and 1/60th (1.66%) of FAS for each year of non-State Police service, capped at 50% of FAS. Social Security Coverage: Yes	Average of 36 highest consecutive months. Includes overtime earned in the period, holiday pay, longevity bonuses earned in the 36-month period, and payment for sick leave in excess of 165 days.	3%
New York State and Local Retirement System: State and Local Police and Firefighters Tier 6: 20-year plan and 25 years plan, effective for members who joined after 4/1/12	Local governments' police and fire employees	20 years of service in plan or other specified police or military service (depending on local government's choice of plan). 25 year-plan has similar provisions based on 25 years of service Vesting: 10 years	65 with less than 20 or 25 years of service, depending on local government's choice of plan	Unchanged from above, except for substitution of age 63 for age 62 in the paragraph above Social Security Coverage: Yes	Average of 60 highest consecutive months with a 10% anti-spiking provision and overtime limited to $15,000 in 2012. FAS is capped at the governor's salary ($179,000 in 2012).	Employee contributions would be required for entire career based upon the member's gross salary (not including excludable overtime), as follows: 3% for those earning $45,000 or less; 3.5% for those earning $45,001 up to $55,000; 4.5% for those earning $55,001 up to $75,000; 5.75% for those earning $75,001 up to $100,000; and 6% for those earning over $100,000
North Carolina Retirement Systems	Firemen's and Rescue Squad Workers' Pension Fund	55/20; Members must contribute to plan for 20 years to receive a benefit.		$170 per month after 20 years Social Security Coverage: Yes	N/A	$10 per month
North Carolina Retirement Systems	Local law enforcement officers	55/5; Any/30 Vesting: 5 years	50/15 Reduced benefit will apply. Vested benefit at 55/5	1.85% times FAS times years of service Social Security Coverage: Yes	Average of 4 consecutive highest years of salary plus accrued annual leave	6%
North Carolina Retirement Systems	State Law Enforcement Officers—state employees with the power of arrest	55/5; Any/30 Vesting: 10 years (member on or after 8/1/11); 5 years (member before 8/1/11)	50/15 Reduced benefit will apply. Vested benefit at 55/5	1.85% times FAS times years of service Social Security Coverage: Yes	Average of 4 consecutive highest years of salary plus accrued annual leave	6%
North Dakota Public Employees' Retirement System	Highway Patrol Retirement System	55; Rule of 80 Vesting: 10 years	50/10	3.6% times FAS times service for first 25 years worked plus 1.75% times FAS for additional years worked Social Security Coverage: No	Average of 36 highest of last 180 months worked	11.3%
North Dakota Public Employees' Retirement System: Law Enforcement Retirement Plan	State and local law enforcement and correctional employees	55/3 continuous years of service; Rule of 85 Vesting: 3 years	50/3 continuous years of service	2% times FAS times years of credited service Social Security Coverage: Yes	Average of 36 highest of last 180 months worked	4.5%

41

Ohio Police and Fire Pension Fund	Local governments' police and fire employees	48/25; 62 with between 15 and 25 years of service Vesting: 15 years	N/A	2.5% times FAS for first 20 years, plus 2% times FAS for years 21 through 25, plus 1.5% times FAS years 26 through 33; Capped at 72% of FAS Social Security Coverage: No	Average of 3 highest years	10%
Ohio Public Employees' Retirement System: Law Enforcement Division	Law Enforcement Officers: state and local employees whose primary duties are to preserve the peace, to protect life and property and to enforce the laws of Ohio, including state Highway Patrol	48/25; 62/15 Vesting: 5 years	N/A	2.5% times FAS times years of service for the first 25 years, plus 2.1% times FAS for each year of service thereafter; The benefit cannot exceed 90% of FAS. Social Security Coverage: No	Average of 3 highest years	11.6%
Ohio Public Employees' Retirement System: Law Enforcement Division	Public Safety Officers: state and local employees whose primary duties other than the law enforcement responsibilities described above, including various court and other institutional employees	Age 52; 62/15 Vesting: 5 years	Age 48 with 25 years of service Benefit reduction will apply for each year age is below 52.	2.5% times FAS times years of service for the first 25 years, plus 2.1% times FAS for each year of service thereafter; The benefit cannot exceed 90% of FAS. Social Security Coverage: No	Average of 3 highest years	11.0%
Oklahoma Firefighters Pension and Retirement System	Paid and volunteer firefighters of participating districts	20 years of service Vesting: 10 years	N/A	Paid: 2.5% times FAS times years of service to a maximum of 30 years Volunteers: $7.53 per month for each year Social Security Coverage: No	Average of 30 highest consecutive months of last 60 months	Paid Members: 8% Volunteer Firefighters: no contribution
Oklahoma Law Enforcement Retirement System	Highway Patrol, Capitol Patrol, other state and university law enforcement officers	62/10; 20 years of service Vesting: 10 years	N/A	2.5% times FAS times years of creditable service Social Security Coverage: Highway Patrol—No; Other Members—Yes	Average of 30 highest consecutive months	8%
Oklahoma Police Pension and Retirement System	Municipal police officers	20 years of service Vesting: 10 years	50/10	2.5% times FAS times years of creditable service Social Security Coverage: Yes	Average of 30 highest consecutive months of last 60 months	8%
Oklahoma Public Employees' Retirement System: Plan for Hazardous Duty Employees	Corrections Security Officers and Pardon & Parole Officers; specified others	62/6; 20 years of service in plan; Rule of 90 Vesting: 6 years	55/10 Benefit reduction will apply.	2.5% times FAS times years of service in plan plus 2% times FAS times years of other creditable service Social Security Coverage: Yes	Average of highest 3 years of the last 10 years in service	8%
Oregon Public Service Retirement Plan Hybrid plan. Details refer to DB component benefits	State and local government police, other law enforcement, and firefighters	Age 60; Age 53 with 25 or more years of service, including 5 years of service immediately preceding retirement Vesting: 5 years	Age 50, but must have 5 years of service immediately preceding retirement.	1.8% time FAS times years of creditable service; In addition, members have DC accounts to which 6% of salary is contributed by employees or picked up by employers Social Security Coverage: Yes	Higher of (1) Average of last 36 months, or (2) the 5 years in which an employee was paid the highest total salary, even if one year was an incomplete calendar year.	Hybrid plan. No member contribution to DB component. Employee contribution of 6% to DC component, which employers may pick up.
Pennsylvania State Employees' Retirement System: Classes of Service A-3 and A-4, effective 1/1/11. See note.	Enforcement officers, corrections officers, psychiatric security aides, Delaware River Port Authority and Capitol police and park rangers	55/20 years of credited service in the classification; Rule of 92 with a minimum of 35 years of credited service Vesting: 10 years	10 years of credited service (vesting requirement) Benefit reduction will apply.	2% or 2.5% times FAS times years of creditable service. The multiplier is determined by the member's choice of Plan A-3 or A-4. Plan A-4 has a higher contribution requirement. Social Security Coverage: Yes	Highest average compensation received during any three non-overlapping periods of four consecutive calendar quarters	A-3: 6.25% to earn a benefit multiplier of 2% A-4: 9.3% to earn a benefit multiplier of 2.5% Employees choose between the plans at beginning of employment; A-3 is the default. Within limits, required employee contributions can be adjusted according to actuarial requirements for funding the plan.
Pennsylvania State Employees' Retirement System: State Police Officers Classes of Service A-3 and A-4 See note.	State Police Officers	20 years of credited service Vesting: 10 years	10 years of credited service Benefit reduction will apply.	For 20 to 25 years of credited service, 50% of highest year's earnings For 25 years of service or longer, 75% of highest year's earnings Social Security Coverage: No	Highest year of service (excludes the last calendar year of service).	A-3: 6.25% to earn a benefit multiplier of 2% A-4: 9.3% to earn a benefit multiplier of 2.5% Employees choose between the plans at beginning of employment; A-3 is the default. Within limits, required employee contributions can be adjusted according to actuarial requirements for funding the plan.
Rhode Island Retirement Security Act of 2011 Hybrid plan	Provisions for municipal fire and police members of the state retirement plan	DB component: 55/25 Current employees aged at least 45 with 10 years of service may retire at 52. Vesting in DB plan: 5 years. For members without Social Security and in DC plan: 3 years for employer contributions to DC; immediately for employee contributions to DC.	N/A	2% times FAS times years of service Social Security Coverage: No	Average of 5 highest consecutive years	DB Component: With COLA option: 8% With no COLA option:7% DC Component: 3%
Rhode Island State Police Retirement Benefits Trust	State police	When benefit reaches 50% of FAS; mandatory when benefit reaches 65% of FAS Vesting: 5 years	N/A	2% times FAS times years of service Social Security Coverage: No	Average of 5 highest years	8.75%
South Carolina Retirement System: Police Officers Retirement System As of 7/1/12	State and local police, firefighters, coroners, magistrates and probate judges	27 years, 5 years of which must be earned service credit; Age 55 with 8 years of earned service credit Vesting: 8 years	N/A	2.14% times FAS times years of service Social Security Coverage: Yes	Average of 20 highest consecutive quarters of earned compensation	Beginning 7/1/2012: 7.3% Beginning 7/1/2104: 13%

South Dakota Retirement System	Class B Public Safety Membership: state law enforcement officers, municipal police and firefighters, county sheriffs, correctional staff, parole agents, campus security conservation officers, and park rangers.	55/ 3 years of earned service credit; Rule of 75 with minimum age of 45 Vesting: 3 years	45/ 3 years of earned service credit Benefit reduction will apply.	2.4% times FAS times years of service before 7/1/02, plus 2.0 % times FAS times years of service after 7/1/02 Social Security Coverage: Yes	Average of highest 12 consecutive calendar quarters in the last 40 quarters of covered employment	8%
Tennessee Consolidated Retirement System	Highway Patrol, wildlife officers, specified other state law enforcement personnel	Age 60 with 5 years of service; Any age with 30 years of service; Mandatory retirement at age 60 Vesting: 5 years	55/25 Benefit reduction will apply.	1.575% times FAS times years of service plus (if FAS is above the Social Security integration level: $46,200 in FY 2006) 1.8375% from the excess times years plus bridge payment until recipient reaches Social Security eligibility at age 62 of 0.75% times FAS times years of service; Benefits are capped at 94.5% of FAS. Social Security Coverage: Yes	Average of 5 highest years	Noncontributory
Texas County and District Retirement System Cash-balance Plan	Local government employees	60 or older. Employees choose among plans that include 5-, 8- or 10-year vesting, and may choose various eligibility options including Rules of 75 and 80, and 20- or 30-year eligibility. Vesting: 5, 8 or 10 years depending upon local government's choice of	N/A	Cash-balance plan that provides lifetime annuities based upon the employee's account balance, which includes employee and employer contributions and investment earnings. Benefits will at least equal the retiree's account balance at the time of retirement. Social Security Coverage: Some	N/A	Contribution rate is set by employer and may range from 4% to 7%. Matched by employer at least dollar for dollar, up to $2.50 per employee dollar. Account interest is guaranteed at 7% annually and may be higher. Employers make contributions necessary to fund the plan on an actuarial basis.
Texas Employee Retirement System: Law Enforcement and Custodial Officers' Supplemental Retirement Fund	State law enforcement officers, custodial employees of the corrections system and parole officers or caseworkers	50/20; Rule of 80 with 20 years of service; Service must be in plan. Vesting: 5 years	20 years of service before age 50 Benefit reduction will apply.	2.8% times years of service times FAS Capped at 100% of FAS Social Security Coverage: Yes	Average of 36 highest months	7%
Texas Municipal Retirement System Cash-balance Plan	Local government employees	Employees choose among plans that include 5- or 10-year vesting, and may choose various eligibility options including 60/5 and 6/10, and 20- or 25-year eligibility. Vesting: 5 years or, in fewer municipal plans, 10 years	N/A	Cash-balance plan that provides lifetime annuities based upon the employee's account balance, which includes employee and employer contributions and investment earnings. Benefits will at least equal the retiree's account balance at the time of retirement. Social Security Coverage: Varies by local government	N/A	Contribution rate is set by employer and may range from 5% to 7%, and is matched by employer at least dollar for dollar, up to $2.00 per employee dollar. Account interest is guaranteed at 5% annually and may be higher. Employers make contributions necessary to fund the plan on an actuarial basis.
Utah Retirement System Tier 2 Hybrid Plan As of July 1, 2011, new employees choose between this plan and the one described below. The hybrid is the default.	State and local government public safety and firefighter members	65/4; 62/10; 60/20; Any age/25 Vesting: 4 years	60 with fewer than 25 years of service Benefit reduction will apply to DB plan	Defined Benefit component: 1.5 times FAS times years of service plus distributions from the defined contribution component of the plan Social Security Coverage: State employees—yes; Local employees—varies by local government	Average of 5 highest years	Noncontributory plan, except that if the employer's annual contribution of 12% of employee compensation is inadequate to amortize the liabilities of the DB component of the plan, employees will contribute to make up the shortfall. When the 12% contribution exceeds the actuarial requirements of the DB plan, the excess is deposited in the employee's defined contribution account.
Utah Retirement System Tier 2 Defined Contribution Plan (a 401(k) plan)	State and local governments public safety and firefighter members	401(k) plan regulations apply; Employer contributions are vested after 4 years	401(k) plan regulations apply	401(k) plan regulations apply Social Security Coverage: State employees—yes; Local employees—varies by local government	N/A	Noncontributory; 12% employee contribution
Vermont Municipal Employees Retirement System	Four plans among which employers may choose for groups of employees. See note.	Varies, depending on employer's plan selection: 55/5 or 65/5 Vesting: 5 years	Varies, depending on employer's plan selection, available in most plans	Varies, depending on employer's plan selection, from 1.4% times years of service times FAS to 2.5% times years of service times FAS Social Security Coverage: Yes	Varies, depending on employer's plan selection, from average of 2 highest consecutive years of earnings to 5 highest consecutive years of earnings	6.98%
Vermont State Retirement System Group C Plan	State police officers or public safety employees assigned to law enforcement duties	Age 55; or Age 50 with 20 years of service Vesting: 5 years	Age 50 with 20 years of service No reduction for early retirement	2.5% times years of service times FAS; Benefit is capped at 50% of final average salary. Social Security Coverage: Yes	Average of 2 highest consecutive years of earnings	5%
Virginia Retirement System Enhanced Benefits for Eligible Political Subdivision Hazardous Duty Employees Plan 2 as of 7/1/10	Local government employees: sheriffs, deputies, police, firefighters, EMT's	60/5; 50/25; Mandatory retirement at 70, except for sheriffs, regional jail superintendents and jail farm superintendents Vesting: 5 years	Age 50 with 5 years of credited service Benefit reduction will apply.	Sheriffs and Jail Superintendents: 1.85% times FAS times years of service; Others: 1.7% times FAS times years of service; Employers may select a higher multiplier; Some employees are eligible for a hazardous duty supplement to bridge years between retirement and early Social Security eligibility Social Security Coverage: Yes	Average of 60 highest consecutive months	5%
Virginia Retirement System Law Officers' Retirement System: Plan 2 as of 7/1/10	Various state law enforcement officers, correctional and parole officers; campus police	60/5; 50/25 Vesting: 5 years	Age 50 with 5 years of credited service Benefit reduction will apply.	2% times FAS times years of service Social Security Coverage: Yes	Average of 60 highest consecutive months	5%

Virginia Retirement System State Police Officers' Retirement System Plan 2 as of 7/1/10	State Police officers	60/5; 50/25 Mandatory retirement at 70 Vesting: 5 years	Age 50 with 5 years of credited service Benefit reduction will apply.	1.85% times FAS times years of service plus Hazardous duty supplement paid to those who retire with at least 20 years of hazardous duty service until they are eligible for Social Security. It is not available to those who retire at or after their normal Social Security retirement age. Social Security Coverage: Yes	Average of 60 highest consecutive months	5%
Washington Law Enforcement Officers' and Fire Fighters' Retirement System Plan 2	State, county and municipal sheriffs, police, firefighters, marshals and public safety officers	53/5 Vesting: 5 years	50/20 Benefit reduction will apply. Social Security Coverage: Varies by local government. Yes for about 6% of fire and 58% of police	2% times FAS times years of service	Average of 60 highest consecutive months	Effective 7/1/11: 8.46%
Washington State Patrol Retirement System Plan 2	Full-time officers only	Any/25; 55/Any; Mandatory retirement at age 65 Vesting: 5 years	55 with 5 years of service credit Benefit reduction will apply. Social Security Coverage: No	2% times FAS times years of service; Maximum of 75% of FAS	Average of 60 highest consecutive months	Effective 7/1/11: 6.59%
Washington Public Safety Employees' Retirement System Plan 2	State and local employees whose jobs contain a high degree of physical risk, but who are not eligible for the Law Enforcement Officers' and Fire Fighters' Retirement System (LEOFF)	65/5 60/10 Vesting: 5 years	53/20 Benefit reduction will apply. Social Security Coverage: Yes	2% times FAS times years of service	Average of 60 highest consecutive months	Effective 7/1/11: 6.36%
Wisconsin Retirement System	Protective Employees covered by Social Security; state police, other state and local public safety employees	53/25; 54 with less than 25 years of service Vesting: 5 years	50 Benefit reduction will apply. Social Security Coverage: Yes	2% times years of service times FAS. An alternative "money purchase" formula is also applied in each case, and the higher benefit of the two results is paid. See note.	Average of 3 highest 3 years need not be consecutive	5.9%
Wisconsin Retirement System	Protective Employees not covered by Social Security; some local government firefighters	53/25; 54 with less than 25 years of service Vesting: 5 years	50 Benefit reduction will apply. Vesting: 5 years	2.5% times years of service times FAS An alternative "money purchase" formula is also applied in each case, and the higher benefit of the two results is paid. See note. Social Security Coverage: No	Average of 3 highest 3 years need not be consecutive	5.9%
Wyoming Retirement System	Game Warden, Highway Patrol and Criminal Investigation Pension Plan	50/6 Vesting: 6 years	N/A Social Security Coverage: Yes	2.5% times FAS times years of service, not to exceed 75% of FAS	Average of 36 highest consecutive months	12.64
Wyoming Retirement System	Law Enforcement Pension Plan: sheriffs, municipal police, corrections system officers and parole agents, and various other state and local law enforcement personnel	60/4 Any/20 Vesting: 4 years	50/4 Social Security Coverage: Some, most police positions are not covered	2.5% times FAS times years of service; not to exceed 75% of FAS	Average of 60 highest consecutive months	8.6%
Wyoming Retirement System	Paid Fire Plan B: local government professional firefighters	50/4 Vesting: 4 years	N/A Social Security Coverage: No	2.8% times FAS times years of service for up to 25 years of service; Benefit is capped at 70% of FAS.	Average of 36 highest consecutive months	8.5%

Note. Table 1 reflects the most recent state governments' public safety retirement plans for all 50 states in the United States as they are listed on the National Conferences of State Legislatures (NCSL) database. Some states have multiple listings that reflect individuals filling different roles and jobs or multiple plans available to different people.

The data provided in Table 1 reflects the significant heterogeneity that exists between states where police officers' retirement benefits and pensions are concerned (NCSL, n.d.). Some states require officers to serve a certain number of years before collecting benefits, while others do not. Some states specify a minimum age to collect retirement benefits, while others do not. Some states include employee contributions in their retirement benefits, while other states do not offer this feature. Social security benefits are allotted in addition to retirement benefits in some states, while in other states retired officers receive either a pension or their social security benefits. Further, the actual formula used to compute retirement benefits based on final actual salary (FAS) and other factors varies widely between states, as does the formula used to compute the FAS. Thus, while retirement preparation and financial planning are necessary for police officers working in any state, the state an officer was employed by can significantly impact their available financial resources during retirement and the degree of planning necessary to ensure financial well-being through the whole span of retirement.

In the state of Kentucky, where my study is based, there is a single retirement system that is responsible for the retirement benefits of state police in addition to state or county employees who perform hazardous duties (NCSL, n.d.). According to the NCSL database information shown in Table 1, police officers are eligible for retirement after 20 years of service and/or at the age of 55 after serving in a hazardous services capacity for at least 5 years. To fulfill the requirements for early retirement with reduced benefits, officers must be age 50–54 with at least 15 years serving in a hazardous services capacity or 55+ with fewer than five years serving in a hazardous services capacity. The benefit formula for Kentucky is social security coverage + 2.5% × FAS × years of service. The FAS in Kentucky is computed by averaging the three highest salaries earned by an employee across a span of at least 24 months of service. Employees contribute 8% of their earnings. Compared to other states, Kentucky's retirement benefits for police officers and how they are computed are relatively generous and easier to acquire in some ways. The computation of the FAS using the three highest earned salaries, rather than an average of earnings from 50 or more months like many other states, benefits officers. Further, many other states that offer full benefits before the age of 60 require 25 years of service or more, making early retirement potentially more accessible for officers who have served in a hazardous services capacity for five or more years.

Retirement, particularly from jobs characterized by shift work and long-term commitment to an organization, should not be a process that individuals take on by themselves (Spraggins, 2019). Many individuals nearing retirement age perceive that they are about to embark on a journey alone that will not be understood by others who are not retired. Others will isolate instead of seeking help and support from others. Rather, Spraggins (2019) contended that because ample research evidence indicates numerous hardships and challenges that retirees, and retired police officers specifically, are predicted to face, police departments and agencies have an ethical duty to assist with retirement preparation outside of, and in addition to, financial planning. Namely, the researcher emphasized the sense of loss police officers can feel when retiring in addition to a real or perceived loss of social support and mental or physical health issues.

Effective financial planning may make the process and transition more enjoyable and less stressful for retirees. Recent research evidence suggests that effective financial planning before retirement facilitates psychosocial well-being during retirement (Topa et al., 2018). Retirees are more likely to feel secure during retirement if they have enough money to sustain their lifestyle (Dingemans et al., 2017). Some choose bridge employment as a means of supplementing insufficient financial savings (Burkert & Hochfellner, 2017).

Many retirees hire financial advisors to help them plan and enact their financial transition into retirement (Cooper et al., 2018). Despite this, some retirees experience significant negative ramifications as a result of hiring someone who is either poorly trained or has malicious intent. Advisors may intentionally choose ill-advised financial management options with higher fees to their benefit. Choosing the wrong financial management strategies as a result of poor guidance can lead to significant financial hardship for retirees. Many retirees, particularly those who are older, are the target of financial scams (Fenge & Lee, 2018). In the case of police officers and other retirees who receive correspondence and documents pertaining to retirement benefits from multiple sources, it can be difficult to spot scammers who are seeking to mimic official correspondence and obtain sensitive information. In particular, retirees who have physical or mental disabilities, poor financial literacy, and/or other vulnerabilities are at a higher risk of being taken advantage of by retirement advisors (Cooper et al., 2018). Thus, the individuals involved with one's financial planning process for retirement can have as much of an impact on financial management during retirement as the planning itself.

While financially planning for retirement is a relatively straightforward process, the same does not go for planning for the nonfinancial aspects of the transition (Abdulkadir et al., 2018). Interestingly, an internet search of information on *police officer retirement in the United States* almost solely returned results pertaining to pensions and retirement benefits. This search yields further evidence that retirement planning and preparation resources for police officers in the United States often focus on the financial planning aspect, with less attention being paid to other factors that impact retirement satisfaction and quality of life during retirement.

Preretirement counseling is an evidence-supported method of seeking to mitigate any negative psychological consequences of retirement. Numerous approaches to preretirement counseling have been developed, some of which are tailored to retirees leaving specific career fields. According to Abdulkadir et al. (2018), preretirement counseling can lessen the likelihood of: "i. Postretirement shock and health problems, ii. Negative stereotype ideas associated with retirement, [and] iii. Dissatisfaction with retirement and tendency to miss ones' previous job routine" (p. 15).

Through preretirement counseling, retirees can also become more aware of certain challenges they may face, allowing them to address them in a supportive clinical environment. Abdulkadir et al. (2018) developed the following recommendations for a comprehensive and effective approach to retirement counseling:

1. Retirement talks either in groups or individually to potential retirees.

2. Since retirement is not restricted to finance but also concerns adequate use of leisure time, social interaction and mental alertness or mind activeness, all these areas must be addressed by a qualified counsellor who specialises in retirement issues to adequately take care of the needs of retirees appropriately.

3. The retirement counselling must take into cognizance, the self-control methods to help individuals increase personal control over their own behavior that could cause them stressful conditions.

4. Another area is introducing social modelling observational learning effects, self-study and thought suppression to retirees.

5. Workers must be helped through classical aversion conditioning. (p. 21)

Not all preretirement counseling is created equal; thus, evidence-based recommendations developed by researchers such as Abdulkadir et al. (2018) help to inform counseling methods and approaches that address common retirement experiences and challenges.

Preretirement counseling also serves to bring awareness to the importance of retirement planning among retirees who may not have sought out resources on their own if they were not discussed during counseling (MacKenzie, 2017). The process of finding useful retirement resources and making numerous retirement-related decisions alone can be daunting; thus, preretirement counseling is an option that provides professional guidance and a second opinion. Onijigin (2020) found a significant positive relationship between the extent of retirement planning and participation in retirement counseling among a sample of 300 retired civil servants. During another recent study, Olatomide (2017) found that both preretirement counseling and family involvement had significant and positive effects on how retirees adjusted to retirement. Gathiira et al. (2019) found that participation in retirement counseling programs with a psychosocial focus could help mitigate the negative implications of participants' lack of preparedness for retirement. Among 334 working professionals representing a larger sample who participated in a retirement counseling program with a psychosocial focus, participants' preparedness for retirement was found to significantly increase following program completion (Gathiira et al., 2019). These findings reinforce the value of retirement counseling across a wide demographic of retirees.

Summary

To reiterate, this research was aimed at addressing the psychosocial difficulties many police officers experience during retirement (Bullock et al., 2018). In response to this problem, the purpose of this qualitative phenomenological study was to explore how retired police officers perceive their psychosocial experiences during their retirement. The theoretical framework of this research was informed by the theory of continuity and the role theory of retirement. Phenomenological interviews with retired police officers were the source of data that informed how the research questions and research problem were addressed.

Retirement, and the transition to retirement in particular, is complex and influenced by a multitude of factors (Landon & Ritz, 2016). Retirement is characterized by a significant amount of change, to which people respond very differently (Henning et al., 2016). Researchers have revealed significant heterogeneity in responses to the retirement transition process based on demographic characteristics such as gender, education, and occupational status. The principles of the theory of continuity suggest that retirees should aim to maintain similarities between the internal and external structural aspects of their lifestyle before and after retiring, while principles of the role theory of retirement help to explain why it is beneficial for retirees to adopt new roles and activities to replace their working role during retirement (Atchley, 1989; van Ingen & Wilson, 2017).

Some of the most commonly-cited factors that impact retirement adjustment and outcomes include mental health, physical health, social support, financial resources, planning and preparation, type of retirement, and occupation before retirement. These relationships vary considerably. Social support, for instance, has been shown to have a significant moderating effect on other factors that directly impact retirement outcomes, including access to financial resources and whether retirement is voluntary or involuntary.

Certain retirement experiences and challenges are more prevalent among former police officers than retirees in general. These include certain mental or physical health conditions, a significant sense of loss related to their previous role, and a loss of social support and camaraderie among fellow officers with relatable experiences (Hope, 2017; Marchand et al., 2015; Nho & Kim, 2017). Despite certain disadvantages during retirement, many police officers also have access to certain retirement resources that are not afforded to most retirees.

Retirement benefits for police officers, including if or when officers can access partial early retirement benefits, vary significantly state to state in the United States (NCSL, n.d.). While retirement advisors can be a helpful asset for retirees seeking to navigate the process of managing their finances, some are predatory and seek to add unexplained fees or otherwise take advantage of unsuspecting retirees (Fenge & Lee, 2018). Retirement counseling and careful retirement planning are two strategies that researchers have found to mitigate the likelihood of significant challenges before, during, and after the transition to retirement.

In response to this literature review, the following research questions were posed:

RQ1: How do retired police officers perceive their own psychosocial experiences during their retirement?

RQ2: What factors positively impact the retirement of police officers?

RQ3: What factors negatively impact the retirement of police officers?

Chapter 3 provides details of the research methods I selected for this qualitative phenomenological study. I also provide information including the selected research design, sample selection strategy, and research analysis approach. A summary concludes the chapter.

CHAPTER 3:

Research Method

The purpose of this phenomenological study was to explore how retired police officers perceive their psychosocial experiences during their retirement and the positive and negative factors that impact their retirement. The phenomenon that served as the focus of this study was the psychosocial experiences of police officers during their retirement. The unit of analysis was the individual experiences and perceptions of police officers who are currently in retirement voluntarily. Previous studies have largely focused on quantitative studies, which has helped to identify some of the limitations in the literature. Through this qualitative study, however, I sought an in-depth understanding of how some of the known factors are actually experienced in individuals, how these factors interact, and how additional unknown factors may contribute to the lived experiences of retired police officers.

This chapter includes an in-depth discussion of my study's research methods. The sections included in the chapter are the following: (a) research design and rationale, (b) role of the researcher, (c) methodology, (d) issues of trustworthiness, and (e) ethical issues. The chapter ends with a summary of the most important descriptions of the research methods.

Research Design and Rationale

Phenomenological research was used to understand the lived experience of retired police officers regarding their transition to retirement, perceptions of their changing roles, any psychological problems and difficulties experienced during this period, and the positive and negative experiences that impact their retirement. Phenomenological research is the systematic exploration of the lived experience of individuals, which is subjective in nature (Moustakas, 1994). Phenomenological research is focused on interpreting the internal experiences of a group of individuals as a method of understanding a complex phenomenon.

A case study was not appropriate for this study because this research design is used when a phenomenon is tied to a specific context, highlighting their interconnectedness with each other (Yin, 2017). Moreover, sources such as documents, archival records, and observations would not have been effective in capturing the lived experience and informed perceptions of the individuals given the nature of the process involved in these data collection methods. Even though the use of multiple sources is a strength of case studies (Yin, 2017), in-depth semistructured interviews through a phenomenological approach were more consistent with the goals of exploring the lived experience and informed perceptions of retired police officers.

Grounded theory would not have been an appropriate selection for this study because this research design is primarily used as an instrument for the development of theories about a particular phenomenon (Glaser & Strauss, 2017). Even though the results of my study may be instrumental in the development of theory, the production of theories was not the purpose of my study. Rather, the purpose was more focused on the lived experience and informed perceptions of a group of individuals who were currently exposed to the same phenomenon, which was retirement.

Ethnography was also not an appropriate research design because this qualitative design is more appropriate in culture-based studies that require intensive immersion from the researcher (Madden, 2017). Even though retired police officers can be considered a unique group, they do not constitute as an ethnic or cultural group. The nature of the involvement I had with the participants, which was through semistructured interviews, did not rise to the deep immersion often required in ethnographic research studies (Madden, 2017).

A phenomenological research study was more consistent with studying the lived experience and informed perceptions of retired police officers using semistructured interviews. The selection of phenomenological research design was appropriate because the exploration of the lived experience of retired police officers required interpretation of their own subjective perspectives and views on retirement. Other groups of individuals, such as their spouses or parents, were not be able to provide the relevant internal processes that were required to understand the lived experiences and informed perceptions of retired police officers.

Role of the Researcher

As the primary investigator, I was both the observer and the collector of data. This means that I was responsible for a wide range of tasks during the course of the study, such as the recruitment of participants and conducting the semistructured interviews. The scope of this role was extended to the transcription and analysis of data in order to minimize the number of individuals who have access to the data.

I did not have any personal or professional relationships with the participants. More importantly, I did not have any supervisory relationship with any of the participants, which prevented any conflict of interests or roles. I am a previous officer, which was beneficial in interacting with other retired police officers. This connection helped me to gain rapport with and support from the participants. This could have also highlighted biases, which were addressed through bracketing (Moustakas, 1994).

Given that I had already read a significant amount of literature on the topic of retirement, certain biases and preconceived ideas may have been present. These preconceived ideas about retirement included the beliefs that preparation is necessary for adaptive retirement, that retirement without social support could be difficult, and that financial security is necessary for smoother transition to retirement. Potential researcher biases were be managed through bracketing, the mindful decision to check preconceived notions in order to prevent interference with the research process (Tufford

& Newman, 2012). Potential power relationships were managed by not recruiting anyone who I had a direct relationship with, whether previous or at the present.

Methodology

In this section, an in-depth discussion of the methodology is provided. The first subsection includes a description of the logic for participant selection. The second subsection focuses on the instrumentation. The third subsection focuses on the recruitment, participation, and the collection of data. The final subsection of the methodology section is the data analysis procedure.

Participant Selection Logic

The population of this study included retired police officers in the northeastern region of the United States. The sample consisted of 10 retired police officers in a large city in a northeastern state in the United States. Twelve participants were expected to be adequate based on the suggestion of experts on the appropriate sample size for qualitative research (Fusch & Ness, 2015; Walker, 2012). Even though data saturation cannot be guaranteed based on a predetermined number of participants, past researchers have indicated that a minimum of 10 participants is often needed in order to reach data saturation (Francis et al., 2010).

A snowball sampling technique was utilized, focusing on selecting participants based on the recommendations or suggestions of the first few individuals who were able to participate in this study. Recruitment involved social media advertisements and posting flyers in local police departments. When purposeful sampling is used to identify the participants in a study, the researcher chooses participants based on their anticipated ability to generate the data needed to answer the research questions (Palinkas et al., 2015). Purposeful sampling was the appropriate sampling technique for this study because qualitative studies give priority in selecting a small number of participants that have direct and deep connections with the phenomenon being explored (Suri, 2011). The sample was comprised of male and female participants in order to acquire a more diverse dataset; however, the sample was confined to recruiting 10–14 participants in order to delve deeper into their individual experiences.

Instrumentation

In qualitative studies, the researcher is the main instrument (Bresler, 2008). Hence, I was responsible for collecting data through semistructured interviews. Even though I utilized NVivo software to manage the data, I remained the main instrument in implementing the steps espoused by Smith (2014) when using the interpretive phenomenological analysis (IPA) method.

Semistructured interviews served as the instrument that led to the data needed for this study. A semistructured interview is both structured and flexible in format, giving researchers the opportunity to ask open-ended questions and unique follow-up or probing inquiries based on the responses of each participant (Chan et al., 2013). The use of semistructured interviews was appropriate in phenomenological studies because participants were encouraged to provide elaborate and detailed answers that reflected their experiences and perspectives without being constrained by a strict format (Chan et al., 2013).

An interview guide was prepared based on careful consideration of the research problem, purpose, framework, and the research questions, serving as the main instrument that was used for the collection of data (see Appendix A). The interview guide contained several open-ended questions intended to elicit rich information about the lived experience of retired police officers regarding their transition to retirement, perceptions of their changing roles, and the psychological problems and difficulties they may have experienced during this period. The interview guide helped me to ask appropriate and relevant questions and maintain some level of consistency in questioning the different participants. The exact flow of the interviews, however, was specific to each participant in order to be consistent with the principle of the semistructured method as a flexible interview technique (Rabionet, 2011).

Procedures for Recruitment, Participation, and Data Collection

Prior to the recruitment of participants and the collection of data, IRB approval was gained to ensure the appropriateness of the study and ensure participants would not be harmed. Recruitment involved social media advertisements and posting local flyers in police departments. When snowball sampling is used to identify the participants in a study, the researcher utilizes the contacts of the initial participants in order to identify more individuals who also qualify to be part of the study (Noy, 2008). Hence, I conducted a brief eligibility check from interested individuals in order to determine whether they qualified to be part of the study (see Appendix B). Specific focus was given to the determination that potential participants needed to have retired voluntarily.

An informed consent form was prepared (see Appendix C), which was used to orient the participants about how data was kept confidential, their ability to withdraw from the study without consequence at any point in time, and the process used to destroy all the data after a predetermined period of time as determined by Walden University. The signatures of the participants on the informed consent forms were required in order to proceed with the data collection through interviews. I discussed the contents of the informed consent form in order to fully explain the terms and declarations stated in said document. No form of compensation was offered to be part of the study.

Semistructured interviews were used to collect data. As previously noted, a semistructured interview is both structured and flexible in format, giving researchers the opportunity to ask open-ended questions and unique follow-up or probing inquiries based on the responses of each participant (Chan et al., 2013). The use of semistructured interviews is appropriate in phenomenological studies because participants are encouraged to provide elaborate and detailed answers that reflect their experiences and perspectives (Chan et al., 2013).

The individual interviews were conducted through Skype or Zoom in order to account for the limitations brought about by COVID-19. The sessions were encrypted in order to protect the confidentiality of the participants. The sessions were audio-recorded in preparation for the transcription and analysis of data. There was no time limit; however, the approximate length of the interview was expected to be less than one hour. After each interview, I reiterated what was stated in the informed consent form regarding the follow-up contact for member checking. More specifically, participants were informed through email to verify the accuracy of the interview transcripts and provide some feedback once the analysis was completed. All further correspondences were confined to email in order to minimize further unnecessary inconvenience for the participants. I conducted interviews until data saturation was reached.

Data Analysis Plan

All the individual interviews were transcribed in preparation for the analysis. After all the transcripts had been generated, member checking was conducted with the participants to ensure the accuracy of the data. After the transcripts were finalized, NVivo software was used for the management of data. NVivo is a software widely used in qualitative studies, intended to store large quantities of data in a single location where various processes can be performed, such as the creation of nodes, visualization of themes, and generation of frequency tables (Bazeley & Jackson, 2013). The software, however, is not be able to perform actual coding processes without the decision-making of a researcher.

To answer the research questions of my study, IPA was utilized, as the goal was to capture the essence of the experiences of the participants by developing themes from the data (Smith, 2014). The steps involved in IPA are the following: (a) looking for themes in the first participant, (b) connecting the themes, (c) continuing the analysis with the other participants, and (d) writing up the essence of the experience of the entire sample (Smith, 2004).

The first step of IPA is the determination of themes from the first participant (Smith, 2004). This stage of the analysis entails reading the transcript multiple times in order to break down the data into smaller units. The process involves assigning comments to a particular portion of text that highlights the unique or significant insight about that text. The researcher then proceeds with identifying themes and contradictions within the same transcript and codes assigned labels that encapsulate their unique meaning (Smith, 2004).

The second stage involves the analysis of the initial list of themes that were developed from the first participant (Smith, 2004). These initial themes are eventually clustered into several categories based on their relationship with each other in terms of thematic content and thematic similarity. At this stage of IPA, several categories are developed with the corresponding themes that were generated for the first participant indicated.

The third step of IPA is the continuation of the analysis with the other participants (Smith, 2004). This stage entails both convergence and divergence from the initial categories and themes from the first participant. Similar themes are subsumed to the previously developed categories, whereas new themes are assigned to newly developed categories. This process of convergence and divergence is repeated until all the participant transcripts have been analyzed.

The final stage of the data analysis is writing up the final report, which details the essence of the phenomenon as perceived and experienced by the participants as a group (Smith, 2004). This stage involves the translation of the themes generated from the analysis into a coherent narrative account. The analysis becomes expansive because themes are explained and illustrated (Smith, 2004). The themes serve as the foundation of the final interpretation of the data represented through a detailed narrative of the experiences of the participants.

Issues of Trustworthiness

The trustworthiness of a qualitative study is important to establish in order to demonstrate the merits of the research as an acceptable scientific inquiry (Amankwaa, 2016; Korstjens & Moser, 2018). The four criteria that establish the trustworthiness of a qualitative study include credibility, transferability, dependability, and confirmability (Korstjens & Moser, 2018). These four criteria of trustworthiness are discussed in this section.

Credibility refers to the correctness of the data and the interpretation of the results, indicating that the findings are true reflections of the participants' experiences and perceptions (Pandey & Patnaik, 2014). Member checks, saturation, reflexivity, and peer review were all utilized. Member checking, through the sending of interview transcripts, was utilized to ensure that the essence of the phenomenon as perceived and experienced by the participants as a group was reflected in the data (Smith, 2004). As stated earlier, data saturation was utilized as a basis for establishing the sufficiency of the sample size in order to demonstrate that the participants in the sample had successfully described the core components of this particular phenomenon (Francis et al., 2010).

Transferability pertains to the external validity of a qualitative study, indicating that the findings have outside utility and relevance (Amankwaa, 2016). Providing thick descriptions and variation in participant selection are the strategies that were utilized to enhance transferability. To enhance the transferability of the findings, I was explicit and detail-oriented about the description of the research context and sample. More specifically, thick descriptions of the particulars of the research study's context facilitated the educated application of the findings outside this current study (Hellström, 2008). Transferability was also enhanced through variation in participant selection, which was ensured by attempting to recruit equal numbers of men and women in the sample in order to ensure that the male and female experiences of retired police officers were represented equally in the study.

Dependability refers to the extent to which the study can be replicated by other researchers (Pandey & Patnaik, 2014). In order to enhance the dependability of my research study, I created an audit trail to document my methodological decisions (Connelly, 2016). I generated an audit trail carefully logging why certain methodological procedures needed to be made, and if deviations had been made, why such modifications were necessary.

Confirmability is the degree to which the study in its entirety can be considered as objective (Korstjens & Moser, 2018). Reflexivity, which is the deliberate process of being transparent with the biases and preconceived notions of the researcher, were used to enhance the confirmability of the study (Jootun et al., 2009). By revealing the personal biases and opinions that are relevant to the research topic, other researchers are given enough information on where the author comes from in terms of initial beliefs about retirement among police officers.

Ethical Procedures

The Institutional Review Board (IRB) application was addressed before any data could be collected. Initial approval from the research site was secured first before lodging the IRB application. I received agreements to gain access to participants by going to several police departments in order to gain access to potential participants, who were retired police officers who had voluntarily left the service. The actual recruitment of participants did not commence until IRB approval had been acquired from the university.

Recruitment involved social media advertisements and posting local flyers in order to reach potential participants who met the eligibility criteria. Ethical concerns related to recruitment materials were addressed by emphasizing the voluntary nature of the study and the fact that no incorrect information was purposefully put in the materials to deceive any individual. I was specific and accurate in the recruitment materials about what participation in the study entailed in order to avoid incorrect assumptions and misunderstandings.

Gaining informed consent of the participants is one of the most important ethical considerations that researchers need to address. Signing the form is often not sufficient to establish informed consent because the researcher needs to make sure that participants understand what they are signing (Flory & Emanuel, 2004). Simple language was used in the informed consent form to help aid in effective communication. I discussed the contents of the informed consent form in order to fully explain the terms and declarations stated in said document.

The option for withdrawal is another important ethical component of any credible research (Wilson et al., 2018). I gave participants the right to withdraw from the study at any point even if initial consent was given and documented. If during the semistructured interview, a participant had expressed the desire to withdraw from the study, I would have honored the request without any further inconvenience.

Confidentiality is another consideration that I needed to address in order to uphold the ethical standards of research. All data was kept in a locked cabinet in order to protect the paper documents from being accessed by other individuals. All electronic data was stored in a password-protected folder and computer so that only I could have access to the files. Real names were also be substituted with random dummy names in order to protect the identities of the participants. Even though the participants were expected to be at more advanced ages, the research was still considered minimal risk given that the nature of the research was confined to conducting individual semistructured interviews. A list of numbers was given in order to gain access to a mental health professional, such as a psychologist, if participants became too agitated or emotional during the interview. After five years have elapsed, all paper documents and electronic data will be permanently and systematically destroyed.

Summary

The purpose of this phenomenological study was to explore how retired police officers perceive their psychosocial experiences during their retirement and the positive and negative factors that impact their retirement. A phenomenological research study is consistent with studying the lived experience and informed perceptions of retired police officers using semistructured interviews. The selection of phenomenological research design was appropriate because the exploration of the lived experience of retired police officers required interpreting their own subjective perspectives and views on retirement.

The sample consisted of 10 retired police officers in a large city in a northeastern state in the United States. A purposeful sampling technique was utilized, which focused on selecting participants who were able to provide rich information about the retirement of police officers (Palinkas et al., 2015). I gained access to potential participants through a recruitment process involving social media advertisements and posting flyers locally.

Semistructured interviews were used to collect data, which gave me the opportunity to be flexible with and probe each participant without being constrained by a strict format or guide (Chan et al., 2013). To answer the research questions of the study, IPA methodology was utilized to analyze the data. The goal of IPA is to capture the essence of the experiences of the participants by developing themes from the data (Smith, 2014). The next chapter contains an in-depth discussion of the results of the data analysis.

CHAPTER 4:

Results

The problem was that researchers had not studied how retired police officers perceive their psychosocial experiences during their retirement and the positive and negative factors that impact their retirement. The purpose of this study was to explore the problem and better understand the psychosocial experiences of retired police officers. Three research questions were used to solve the problem. Those research questions were:

RQ1: How do retired police officers perceive their own psychosocial experiences during their retirement?

RQ2: What factors positively impact the retirement of police officers?

RQ3: What factors negatively impact the retirement of police officers?

This chapter will report the results of the data analysis and how the results were obtained.

This chapter presents the findings from the data. The sections included in this chapter are the following: (a) the setting, (b) demographics, (c) data collection, (d) data analysis, (e) evidence of trustworthiness, and (f) results. The chapter ends with an essence summary of the lived experience of retired police officers regarding their psychosocial experiences in retirement.

Setting

The data were collected from the Fraternal Order of Police (FOP) in Louisville, Kentucky. The FOP is the largest organization of sworn law enforcement officers in the U.S. The FOP is comprised of 2,100 state chapters with more than 355,000 members across the U.S. The Louisville, Kentucky chapter of the FOP provides college benefits, life insurance, travel benefits, educational resources, and financial resources to the members. Participants of this study were members of the FOP chapter 77 in Louisville, Kentucky. Due to the social distancing mandates in the wake of the COVID-19 pandemic, interviews of these participants took place via Zoom.

Demographics

All participants of this study were members of the Louisville, Kentucky chapter of the FOP. As such, all participants were retired law enforcement officers in the state of Kentucky. Three participants were females, and seven participants were males. Six participants identified their race as White and four reported their race as African American. Participants ages ranged from 47 to 52. Given that all participants were retired law enforcement officers, the participants' years of service ranged from 20 to 27 years. Table 2 summarizes the demographic information of the participants' from this study.

Table 2.

Demographics of Interviewed Participants

Participant	Age	Sex	Race	Years of Service
1	52	F	White	27
2	52	M	White	22
3	49	M	White	21
4	47	M	White	21
5	51	M	White	27
6	47	M	White	21
7	53	F	African American	25
8	51	F	African American	23
9	48	M	African American	21
10	48	M	African American	20

Data Collection

Ten semistructured interviews were conducted with the ten different participants described above. To recruit participants, an initial reach out was sent to chapter 77 of the FOP in Louisville, Kentucky, with regards to their willingness to recruit participants for this study. I contacted the FOP via email with information about the purpose of this study and the need to recruit participants who are registered members of the FOP. The FOP agreed to share information regarding my study, and subsequently forwarded my email to all retired police officers in the Louisville chapter. The email provided to potential participants consisted of a brief description of this study and my contact information. Interested participants then reached out to me directly via email. Upon receiving email inquiries from potential participants, I provided additional information about the parameters of participation and the informed consent form. Participants provided their informed consent, and acknowledge that no compensation would be provided for participation in the study. I then scheduled individual interviews with the participants to take place via Zoom. The Zoom interviews were recorded and transcribed in preparation for analysis.

Data Analysis

I analyzed the data using IPA to develop themes in order to capture the essence of the participants' experiences (Smith, 2014). First, I read the first participant's transcript multiple times, noticed emerging themes, and coded the transcript using NVivo. I analyzed each sentence and assigned a code. The first participant's transcript had 47 codes and 148 individual references. During the second stage, I analyzed themes that emerged from codes generated from P1's transcript. I clustered these based on content and separated them into themes based on their significance to each research question.

During the third stage of data analysis, I repeated the process for all other transcripts and noted cases of convergence or divergence. I combined converging themes with themes developed from the first transcript. I initially gave diverging themes their own code. Each successive transcript had both converging and diverging themes. Diverging themes were eventually eliminated if unsupported by following transcripts or made into coded under "other" if determined to be important discrepant cases.

I created five main categories of codes. Those categories were psychosocial experience, positive experiences, negative experiences, other officers, and other. The first three categories were directly related to each research question. The last two were relevant information that may be either a discrepant case or of importance to the lived experience of retired police officers but were not directly related to the research questions. There were initially 546 references, which I finalized into 266 references based on emerging themes for each category. Table 3 summarizes themes corresponding to each research question.

Table 3.

Summary of Themes

Research Question	Themes
RQ1: How do retired police officers perceive their own psychosocial experiences during retirement?	• Transitioning is easier when retirees have post-retirement plans • Retirees are more social and have more time than before they retired • Feeling powerless to help and a loss of identity are challenges for retired police officers • Retired police officers describe their mental health as mostly positive

RQ2: What factors positively impact the retirement of police officers?	• Having more time positively impacts the retirement of police officers.
	• Being less stressed positively impacts the retirement of police officers.
	• Preparing for retirement positively impacts the retirement of police officers.
RQ3: What factors negatively impact the retirement of police officers?	• Missing the job negatively impacts the retirement of police officers
	• Missing coworkers negatively impacts the retirement of police officers
	• Many police officers report no negative aspects to retirement

Evidence of Trustworthiness

Credibility was ensured during data analysis by obtaining saturation of the data. I coded each transcript according to emerging themes and fewer and fewer new themes emerged as I moved on from each participant. It was clear that data saturation was reached when I coded the final transcript because there was very little divergence from established themes.

Results

This section discusses the results and the themes that emerged in response to each research question. Discrepancies are also mentioned where applicable.

Research Question 1: How Do Retired Police Officers Perceive Their Own Psychosocial Experiences During Retirement?

Four themes emerged in response to RQ1 regarding four aspects of the psychosocial experience: the transition into retirement, social aspects, perceived challenges, and mental health. Those four themes were new jobs ease transition, retirees have more time and are more social, a major perceived challenge is feeling powerless to help, and mental health is generally positive. These are summarized in Table 4.

Table 4.

Themes for RQ1

Theme	Subtheme	*n* of participants contributing to subtheme (*N*=10)	*n* of references to subtheme in the data
Theme 1: Transitioning is easier when retirees have post-retirement plans	New jobs help with the transition	7	22
	The transition is easy	9	12
Theme 2: Retirees are more social and have more time than before they retired	Retired police officers have more time than they did before retirement	4	8
	Retired police officers are more social in their retirement	5	7
Theme 3: Feeling powerless to help and a loss of identity are challenges for retired police officers	Feeling powerless to help is a challenge	4	6
	A sense of loss of identity is a challenge	4	5
Theme 4: Retired police officers describe their mental health as mostly positive		6	10

Theme 1: Transitioning is Easier When Retirees Have Post-Retirement Plans

This theme addressed RQ1 and the transitioning aspect of police officers "perceived psychosocial experiences during retirement." All participants talked about their transition from the workplace to retirement, and the two most common subthemes mentioned were having a new job and the transition being easy. Regarding transitioning, P1 said, "I basically had two weeks off between retiring from the police department and then starting my new job." P9 said, "I think my transition has been pretty good."

Subtheme 1. Seven participants mentioned transitioning to a new job a total of 22 times. The jobs were diverse and included positions in the private sector, academia, part-time policing or the police foundation, and coaching. P1 went to the private sector and said it was a positive experience. P10 went to the police foundation and stated: "For me, I went straight from the police department to the police foundation, so in fact, I was vacationing out with the police department when I started. Really, I didn't have any downtime." P3 described their transition to academia saying:

> So, I went back to school, got my education. When I retired, I actually wasn't planning on teaching, but literally right when I announced that I was going to retire, they called me, "Are you available?" and asked if I wanted to teach. So, I had an opportunity to go and teach over there and start a second career."

Retired police officers transitioned into these other careers.

P6 stated, "I had other ventures and job opportunities after my retirement... I had employment prepared for my retirement." While many officers transitioned to work elsewhere, P4 discussed transitioning to part-time police work:

> I'm in a small city. There's about # officers. Most of the officers over there are retired LMPD. I worked last night, and I'm on the light shift, and I didn't even get a run last night, Steve. There's really not...

It's just a very nice neighborhood and it's much, much easier. And I miss working for LMPD in some ways. But yeah, Indian Hills is easy.

Subtheme 2. The second subtheme that emerged regarding transition was retired police officers mostly viewing their experience transitioning as easy and smooth. Five participants mentioned a smooth transition seven times. P4 described their transition as, "At first, it was a little different, but overall, it has been good, I would say, very good." Similarly, P5 stated, "Well, my transition was easy because number one, I had worked 26 years in law enforcement, and it was just a time for me to get away." Further, P9 said, "I think my transition has been pretty good." P1 linked having a new job and with having a smooth transition. P1 said:

> I was ready to go and it did help that I had someplace to go and it's been a great opportunity. I think the situation for me personally would have been very different if I had just walked away and I was sitting at home and just drawing my pension check. I think I'll know that I was ready for that. And I think I would have struggled with that both emotionally and psychologically, but like I said the factors for myself personally, it's worked out very well and like I said I'm happy.

Discrepant Cases. Two participants diverged from theme 1 by describing their transitions as slow or a "big change." P2 said, "I think that transitioning into retirement was sort of a big going from a hundred miles an hour representing 2,000 people in the FOP. And then all of a sudden, I'm not doing that anymore. And retiring as a law enforcement officer as well." P4 said also described the transition as slow and difficult but ultimately arrived at the consensus that retiring was overall a positive thing. P4 said:

> Again, when I retired, I was feeling a little bit lost just for the first few weeks, months, even though I retired and went to a part-time job, which was very nice job. Psychologically, it was a big change, but I adjusted as the months went by. Again, in the big picture, it was a good move.

Theme 2: Retirees are More Social and Have More Time than Before They Retired

This theme addressed RQ1 and the social aspect of police officers' lived psychosocial experience during retirement. Social life was mentioned by all participants a total of 29 times. The two most common things mentioned that factored into their social lives were having more time and being more social in general.

Subtheme 1. Four participants mentioned eight times that having more time during retirement than before retirement influenced their social life. P2 said:

Socially, I was always available now to go to those things. I mean, it was nice, but it was kind of weird because it was, hey, I don't have to work so I can go.

And then also though, I think I've kind of gotten a rut while I was working as far as, these are the few things that I knew I would do socially, just because any other time I'd be working or coaching or something like that. And one of the things I'm glad that I did when I was on the police department was not only have friends that were the police. So, after I retired, I had more time just to spend social time with civilian friends that were outside of law enforcement that I hadn't spent a whole lot of time with because we're always so busy and it works.

P7 also described retirement enabling them to be more social because time previously spent working could be dedicated to social events. They said, "Well, I think retirement gives you an opportunity to do things that you might've passed up on while working, whether it was because you were getting called out or working overtime or just had to be ready to respond."

Subtheme 2. Subtheme 2 emerged in response to Theme 2 and the social aspects of RQ1. Five participants mentioned seven times that they were overall more social after retirement than before retirement. When asked about their social experiences in retirement, P4 said, "They're better." P5 discussed how it is easier to socialize while not being consistently perceived as a police officer. P5 said:

> Social experiences were a lot better because now they must, again, you're not a part of the police department. More people tend to socialize with you and conversate with you moreso when you're retired, than when you were working. Because socializing with you while you're working, even though you're in a private setting, or you're in a social setting with what you would so call friends, they still perceive you as working if they're socializing with you.

Discrepant Cases. Most participants expressed having more of a social life because they had more time. P9, however, said their social life was mostly unchanged and attributed their lack of social life to personal preference. P9 said:

> I've never been one to do a whole lot socially. I do some things, but I'm just not one of those individuals that, for lack of better words, that just like go hang out. I am more inclined to be doing things with individuals that we have more in common, such as church and family and things of that nature, or things involving my son.

Another discrepant case was P10, who discussed no longer being fully accepted in their social circle of fellow police officers. P10 expressed, "I think the hardest part has been that once you retire, we talk about this blue family and this comradery, but, man, once you retire, you're like the in-laws. I mean, technically, yeah, you're still part of the family, but you're not on that inner circle of trust."

Theme 3: Feeling Powerless to Help and a Loss of Identity are Challenges for Retired Police Officers

This theme addressed RQ1 and the perceived challenges of police officers' psychosocial experiences following retirement. Nine participants mentioned some sort of challenge a total of 25 times. The two most common challenges mentioned were feeling powerless and a sense of identity loss.

Subtheme 1. Four participants described a sense of wanting to continue to help and being unable to do so. They mentioned wanting to help situations, police officers, and the community. P3 expressed wanting to help in difficult situations. They said, "You know, not giving it much thought, but actually, I wish I was a police officer right now because that's what we take the job for, to address those tough issues."

P7 discussed wanting to help current police officers. They stated, "I had that desire to be back out on the front line, so to speak, with the men and women I had served on the department with and seeing them go through the things they were going through and realizing that I couldn't be out there with them." P2 elaborated on wanting to help the community, stating, "I should be out there making sure people are safe."

Subtheme 2. A subtheme that emerged regarding challenges retired police officers face was a sense of identity loss. Four participants mentioned a sense of identity loss a total of five times. P4 described this phenomenon by saying, "You took years to get on and you worked so hard to get on, to be a part of that. And you walk away, and a little bit of identity, that was your family and your life. I think that was the biggest thing." Similarly, P10 discussed feeling a void following retiring and searching for something to fill that void. They stated, "You want to have a service, so I think the challenge has been finding something that still meets that need, where you feel like you're making a difference, you feel like you're helping and trying to fill that void."

Discrepant Cases. Many participants mentioned missing aspects of their lives before retirement, but no one admitted personal mental health struggles. A common occurrence was officers discussing struggles of other officers. P1 said, "And if you're not ready to do that [retire] mentally or emotionally, you're going to struggle with it. And I've seen that on multiple occasions with officers and former officers that have retired, and they're not prepared. And I've seen some leave and transition, they get other jobs, but they still have trouble letting go." In addition, P10 said, "Again, I think, honestly, I'm kind of an anomaly where I haven't had some of the struggles that a lot of retirees have had."

Theme 4: Retired Police Officers Describe Their Mental Health as Mostly Positive

Theme 4 addressed the mental health aspects of RQ1 and the perceived psychosocial experiences of retired police officers. Theme 4 is that mental health is perceived as overall good. Six participants mentioned a total of six times that their mental health was good or they felt mentally healthy.

P1 said, "Overall, mentally with retirement and transition away from the police department, I would say overall I'm in pretty good shape mentally." P8 also talked about their overall positive mental health, saying, "My psychological health has always been positive. I've been a positive person as a police officer, and a positive person in the community. And I would describe my psychological health as strictly positive." Additionally, P6 said they could describe their mental health as "pretty healthy."

A few participants went further to say that not only was their mental health overall good, but that it was better now that they are retired. P9 elaborated on their mental health improvement saying,

> I think my psychological health is probably better now within my retirement than while on the police department because it's a very stressful job. And after retiring, a lot of that stress was released, and a lot of things I didn't have to take home with me after I got off work. So, I think right now, my mental health is a lot better.

P2 attributed the vast improvement of their mental health during retirement to less stress. They elaborated:

> To be honest, I think it was probably an improvement. There's a lot of stress in everyday policing for those that are in uniform and on the beat or wherever the case might be as well. But there was also a lot of stress when you know that your job is to negotiate collective bargaining agreements with the city to make sure that officers have due process or when they're involved in critical incidents that they're properly represented because they've been putting in life-threatening situations that had to take action and things like that… So, you always feel I don't want to miss something. I don't want to forget something and not do my due diligence. I think that not having all of that stress was probably, I would consider it a sort of an improvement to my psychological wellbeing.

Discrepant Cases. Participant 3 had a different perspective than the majority of participants. They emphasized that being a police officer was not their identity and that was helpful in their retirement experience. P3 said:

> I hear a lot of guys, the ones who retire and say, "I'm not going to do anything," and I'm like, "Yeah, right." You know, I said, I give you about six months, at the longest a year, and you're going to find something to do. And nine times out of 10, six months to a year, they're looking for something to do. They miss police work. They can't let the badge go. I never wanted my identity as a person to be tied to any role that I played, letting that badge go, losing that power, losing that authority, that bothers some people. It didn't bother me at all.

Research Question 2: What Factors Positively Impact the Retirement of Police Officers?

The three themes that emerged in response to RQ2 were having more time in retirement is a positive factor, dealing with less stress is positive, and being prepared for retirement positively impacts the experience. Themes for RQ2 are summarized in Table 5.

Table 5.

Themes for RQ2

Theme	*n* of participants contributing to subtheme (*N*=10)	*n* of references to subtheme in the data
Theme 5: Having more time positively impacts the retirement of police officers	6	8
Theme 6: Being less stressed positively impacts the retirement of police officers	4	7
Theme 7: Preparing for retirement positively impacts the retirement of police officers	2	4

Theme 5: Having More Time Positively Impacts the Retirement of Police Officers

Theme 5 addressed RQ2, which referred to positive aspects of retirement. Six participants mentioned nine times that having more free time and more time with their family is one of the most positive aspects of retirement. Many participants discussed having more time in general, and control of that time, as a positive retirement experience. When asked about what factors positively impacted their experience, P6 answered, "Being home [and] being able to control my time…" Similarly, P7 answered, "Well, like I said, there's time to do things that you couldn't do or didn't do necessarily while working. So, I think that's the main positive thing." P2 also answered, "Well, one that I've previously mentioned was that is that it does free up your schedule. I got to sit at home and for the first time in 20 whatever years watch the two-minute horse race instead of being [at work] for 14 hours, right?"

Other participants elaborated on Theme 5 by specifying that a positive aspect of retirement was having more time for family. When asked what factors positively influenced their retirement, P4 said, "More time for family and friends and travel and things like that." P5 answered similarly, "The fact that I can spend more time with my family, and there are things that I wanted to do with my family that I could not do while working because of the manpower shortages. You couldn't get off. So, number one is just being able to spend more time with my family and doing what I wanted to do."

Participant 7 emphasized Theme 5 and how having more time, particularly more time for family, was the main positive aspect of retirement. P7 said:

There's time to do things that you couldn't do or didn't do necessarily while working. So, I think that's the main positive thing. You can do some more things social with various friends and spend more time with family. Quite often, our families as law enforcement officers suffer. And they realize that. They accept that burden of giving us to the community at times, so to speak. So, I think that's a tremendous thing in having more time with family.

Participant 9 also described in detail how having more time with their family was the thing that positively impacted their retirement the most. They said:

Being a single [parent], one thing that I did not want to do was take additional time away from my young [child]. And so, since I had the time on the department to be able to retire, to me, it was better for me to retire, and be able to have access to my pension, and if I needed to work, I could work part time, and still be involved in my [child's] life, instead of staying on the job and then working extra jobs, taking additional time away from him. I didn't want to do that. So, the main factor was making sure that I was there for my [child]. You're not on that inner circle of trust.

Theme 6: Being Less Stressed Positively Impacts the Lives of Retired Police Officers

Theme 6 addressed RQ2—factors that positively influence the retirement of police officers. Four participants mentioned seven times that being less stressed or worried was a positive experience of retirement. P2 went into detail about how life is less stressful in retirement. They said:

> So, I think one of the positive things was not having the stress all the time of making sure I had all my stuff, and you're always in that, not the red zone, but that orange zone where you're the police and you have to be ready to handle anything at any time. And so that kind of was able to relax. That was positive. It was a positive thing knowing that, okay, whatever I decide to do, whether it's go back to work or not go back to work or whatever I'm going to do, I've completed that first step and I've retired from it now.

> So, I know that what I was promised, I'm going to have that coming in so that I don't have... It's a little different not worrying when you have 11 years on, but what if I get hurt or shot and I can't work anymore? What am I going to do?

P4 said Theme 6 was a bigger positive than Theme 5. They described how having more time with family was a positive but emphasized that less stress was the most important factor. P5 said, "But stress is the number one thing. It's less stressful, so that's positive for me."

Participants described less stress due to a variety of factors. P5 reflected on past experiences and the stress they caused. They described their thankfulness for no longer having to deal with such issues in retirement. They said, "when you think about it and you just look at everything that you've gone through, you just really feel blessed that you don't have the stress, and you don't have to deal with all the issues."

In response to what factors positively influence retirement, P6 elaborated on less worry. They said:

being able to not have certain responsibilities that I had before that at the time I retired as a sergeant, which every day I had to worry, not just about my career, but others that were underneath me. Those things weigh real heavily because everyone that you work with have things that you personally have to deal with. I do realize that at this time it was a relief being able to retire and not have those responsibilities, which I think helps your health.

Theme 7: Preparing for Retirement Positively Impacts the Retirement of Police Officers

Theme 7 addressed RQ2, which asks what factors positively impact the retirement of police officers. Being prepared was mentioned as contributing to a positive retirement experience four times. P10 described preparing themselves mentally for retirement. They said, "Again, of course, I taught a retirement class, so I knew what to expect, so I had stayed on the front end of it. I have read all the studies about how officers really struggle mentally in retirement, so I've made a conscious effort to not fall into that trap." They went on to say, "I think me doing the research and teaching that retirement class and knowing what the statistics were and how they were not very good for us in retirement and making that conscientious effort to avoid those pitfalls, I think was very positive."

Participant 3 talked about being prepared for experiences postretirement and how that positively impacted their experience. They said, "You've got to have some idea, or at least, even if you don't know exactly what you're doing, you have to kind of get things in the works, that if something comes up, you're ready for it" They went on to say, "My preparation prepared me to go for something else."

As previously mentioned, many participants described others' experiences rather than their own. P1 discussed how many officers, but not them personally, are unprepared for retirement. P1 said, "I've also seen people that they get out and they honestly have not prepared themselves for how to go out and find a job in the private sector... I think people have difficulties with retirements because they're not mentally and emotionally ready to leave and they haven't prepared themselves for retirement."

Finally, P4 described the importance of being financially prepared for retirement. They elaborated:

And I think that planning, and I may have planned haphazardly and everything's kind of worked out for me, but looking back, the better you plan for your retirement, what you're going to do, and I think talking with other people that have retired and seeing how they handled it or what they're doing. I think that planning for after retirement is very important, other than just going and saying, "Well, I'm done," and you don't have a plan. I think that's where people get into trouble or maybe it's not what they thought it was. So, I think that's the biggest thing, having a plan.

Research Question 3: What Factors Negatively Impact the Retirement of Police Officers?

The three themes that emerged in response to RQ3 were that missing being a police officer negatively impacted the retirement experience, missing coworkers also negatively impacted retirement, and that there were no viewed negative impacts. These themes are summarized in Table 6:

Table 6.

Themes for RQ3

Theme	*n* of participants contributing to subtheme (*N*=10)	*n* of references to subtheme in the data
Theme 8: Missing the job negatively impacts the retirement of police officers	7	18
Theme 9: Missing coworkers negatively impacts the retirement of police officers	4	5
Theme 10: Many police officers report no negative aspects of retirement	4	5

Theme 8: Missing the Job Negatively Impacts the Retirement of Police Officers

Theme 8 addressed RQ3, which referred to negative aspects of retirement. Seven participants referenced missing the job or some other aspect of being an active police officer as a negative factor a total of 18 times. This theme was referenced three times more than any other theme that addressed RQ3.

P10 said, "I have to be honest, I mean, there are times where just you really miss it." Similarly, P5 said, "But I tell you... you miss it because you know, when you a part of it, you are in the know of everything. So, you really kind of miss the excitement. You miss the energy." P3 related missing policing to missing anything you once loved. They said,

If you love something and you leave it, you're going to miss it. Just like somebody who retired from major league baseball or football, whatever, they miss it. But you know, it's not, for some of them, they got a life outside of that and they move forward. Just another change.

Theme 8 represents missing the job as a negative factor in retirement. When asked what factors negatively impacted their retirement, P6 said, "missing the responsibility of being able to go and know that you're doing something good." Participant 2 offered insight on how missing the job and routine negatively impacts retirement. They provided a personal anecdote and said:

So, regardless how ready I was or how much time I took to make the decision, I did miss, I felt I should be going to work. So, it feels weird that you feel this can't be right. Surely, I'm supposed to be somewhere. Somebody is waiting for me to show up. You just getting those routines. I would find myself driving down the street. And if I wasn't paying attention, I would end up at the firehouse where I used to have to park my car because I live out of county. What am I doing here? I don't have a police car to pick up anymore.

Theme 9: Missing Coworkers Negatively Impacts the Retirement of Police Officers

Theme 9 addressed RQ2—negative factors that impact the retirement of police officers. Four participants mentioned missing coworkers a total of five times. P1 distinguished between missing work (Theme 8) and missing people (Theme 9). They described missing people as the main thing that has had a negative impact on their retirement. P1 said, "I guess from the regrets side mentally was missing the people. I miss the work somewhat, but I miss the people that I work with probably more than anything and that was it."

Participants mentioned missing solidarity with other police officers. P10 said, "I think the hardest part has been that once you retire, we talk about this blue family and this comradery, but, man, once you retire, you're like the in-laws." Echoing the idea of missing solidarity, P6 said that "missing the comradery" was a negative aspect of retirement.

Participant 2 went into detail about how relationships changed between former coworkers following retirement. They described the experience as follows:

> So, I don't know if there was a lot of negative things, but I do think that the people that are your acquaintances at work. Close acquaintances, maybe you didn't hang out a ton outside of work, but you saw them every day or worked with them every day. And that didn't happen anymore. It was that you felt you were losing contact with people that you knew for a long time. So that's a little bit part of the difficulty is when it's not somebody that you knew you were going to see anyway, because you hung out all the time or went to the lake together or whatever. It was just people that you're, I'm not going to see them anymore. It's kind of weird.

Theme 10: Many Retired Police Officers Report No Negative Aspects of Retirement

Theme 10 addressed RQ3 and negative factors experienced by retired police officers in retirement. Theme 10 diverged from Themes 8 and 9 and suggested that there are no negative aspects to retirement. Four participants mentioned five times that there were no negative factors regarding their retirement.

When asked what factors negatively impacted their retirement, four participants gave brief answers stating they could not recall anything negative. P8 said, "I really didn't have anything negative affect my retirement. I really didn't." This is similar to what P9 said, "Factors that negatively impacted my retirement? I really can't think of any factors that negatively

83

impacted my retirement." P1 reiterated the idea that there were no negative factors to retirement by saying, "But other than that, there has been no negative or downside through retiring from my perspective." Finally, P3 also said there were no negative factors to retirement, although they qualified their statement saying they wish they had made more money. P3 said, "Oh man. Be honest with you, I can't think of anything other than, with all of our jobs, we wish we could have made a little bit more money."

Summary

I conducted semistructured interviews to understand the psychosocial experiences of retired police officers. Interviews were based around three research questions, and 10 themes emerged in response to those questions from the interviews. Four themes emerged regarding RQ1, how retired police officers perceive their own psychosocial experiences during their retirement. The four areas that emerged to be most important to the psychosocial experience were how officers viewed their transition to retirement, their social life, perceived challenges in retirement, and how they regarded their mental health.

It was common for police officers to have an easy transition to retirement, and new employment usually helped with that transition. Social life benefited from retirement because retirees had more time. Mental health was self-reported to be mostly positive, though challenges also emerged. Challenges associated with retirement were feeling powerless to help others, being unable to contribute, and losing part of their self-identity. Many officers identified strongly as being a police officer and no longer having that title had negative consequences on their psychosocial well-being.

Three themes emerged regarding RQ2, "what factors positively impact the retirement of police officers?" Retired police officers benefited from having more time and less stress during retirement. In addition, they also had a more positive experience if they were emotionally, mentally, and financially prepared.

Three themes emerged regarding RQ3, "what factors negatively impact the retirement of police officers" Some retired officers reported no negatives to retirement. Most retired police officers, however, missed the job, experiences, their co-workers, and/or the overall experience of being a police officer.

This chapter presented results and themes that emerged from the data. In the next chapter, I further analyze these results, interpret findings, and discuss implications. I also use these results to answer the research questions and understand the essence of how retirement positively and negatively impacts the psychosocial experience of retired police officers.

CHAPTER 5:

Discussion, Conclusions, and Recommendations

The purpose of this qualitative, phenomenological study was to explore how retired police officers perceive their psychosocial experiences during their retirements and the positive and negative factors that impact their retirements. Phenomenological research was used in order to generate an understanding of the lived experience of retired police officers regarding their transition to retirement, perceptions of their changing roles, any psychological problems and difficulties experienced during this period, and the positive and negative experiences that impact their retirements. Phenomenological research is the systematic exploration of the lived experience of individuals, which is subjective in nature (Moustakas, 1994); it is focused on interpreting the internal experiences of a group of individuals as a method of understanding a complex phenomenon.

I selected a phenomenological research study in order to remain consistent with studying the lived experience and informed perceptions of retired police officers. The selection of phenomenological research design was be appropriate because the exploration of the lived experience of retired police officers required that police officers interpret their own subjective perspectives and views on retirement. This was determined to be critical for obtaining the level of richness and depth of data necessary to understand how police officers perceive their own retirement experiences. Other groups of individuals, such as their spouses or parents, would not have been able to provide the relevant internal processes that are required to understand the lived experiences and informed perceptions of retired police officers.

The specific phenomenon that served as the subject of exploration in this study was the psychosocial experiences of police officers during retirement. The key concepts that I explored in this study are retirement, the psychosocial factors that define the experiences of former police officers during this phase in their lives, and the positive and negative aspects that affected their retirement. The unit of analysis was at the individual level, focusing on the subjective experiences of each retired police officer in the study. Phenomenology proved to be useful in generating an understanding of each of these key concepts.

The sample consisted of 10 retired police officers in a large city in a northeastern state in the United States. I performed individual semistructured interviews in order to collect data, which gave me the opportunity to be flexible and probe for additional relevant information with each participant without being constrained by a strict format or guide (Chan et al., 2013). To answer the research questions of the study, I utilized IPA methodology; the goal of IPA is to capture the essence of the experiences of the participants by developing themes from the data (Smith, 2014). This approach was shown to be valuable in conceptualizing the phenomena of interest and provide new insight into the retirement experiences of police officers.

Given the fact that the aim of this study was to understand retired police officers based on their own internal meaning of the phenomena, a qualitative phenomenological study proved to be the most appropriate and optimal research design (Moustakas, 1994). The results from this study offer an improved understanding of the different psychosocial challenges that retired police officers experience during retirement. This study should also be instrumental in the development of interventions that help police officers become more positively adjusted in their retirements based on a deeper understanding of their psychosocial experiences.

Ten semistructured interviews were conducted with ten different participants. Participants came from various backgrounds. There were three females and seven males. Six participants were White and four were African American. Participants' years of service ranged from 20 to

27 years and their ages ranged from 48 to 52. The first research question was, "How do retired police officers perceive their own psychosocial experiences during retirement?" The four themes emerged in response to the first research question regarding four aspects of the psychosocial experience: the transition into retirement, social aspects, perceived challenges, and mental health. The four themes were: new jobs ease transition, retirees have more time and are more social, a major perceived challenge is feeling powerless to help, and mental health is generally positive. These themes were found to be novel and helped extend the research presented in Chapter 2, which is be discussed in the following section.

The second research question was, "What factors positively impact the retirement of police officers?" The three themes that emerged in response to the second research question were: having more time in retirement is a positive factor, dealing with less stress is positive, and being prepared for retirement positively impacts the experience. Finally, the third research question was, "What factors negatively impact the retirement of police officers?" The three themes that emerged in response to the third research question were: missing being a police officer negatively impacted the retirement experience, missing coworkers also negatively impacted retirement, and that there were no viewed negative impacts.

The remainder of this chapter includes a discussion of these findings and conclusions that I drew based on their alignment with literature and theory presented in Chapter 2. An interpretation of the findings is presented first, followed by limitations that may have influenced trustworthiness. Recommendations are then made for future practice and research. Implications are then drawn for positive social change, as well as methodological issues, theory, and practice. This chapter concludes with a summary and outline of key points.

Interpretation of the Findings

This section includes an interpretation of the main findings of this study. This section is centred on the three research questions and the major themes that emerged. Each research question and major theme is presented, and discussion emphasizes alignment with findings presented in the literature identified in Chapter 2. Additionally, the relationship between these findings and the conceptual framework identified in Chapter 1 is discussed.

The first research question was, "How do retired police officers perceive their own psychosocial experiences during retirement?" The four themes emerged in response to RQ1 regarding four aspects of the psychosocial experience were: the transition into retirement, social aspects, perceived challenges, and mental health. The four themes were: new jobs ease transition, retirees have more time and are more social, a major perceived challenge is feeling powerless to help, and mental health is generally positive. There were also several subthemes that emerged within these four main themes, which I described in Chapter 4.

The results related to the first question generally aligned with the literature that was identified and synthesized in Chapter 2. Specifically, numerous researchers have previously analyzed the psychosocial experiences of retirees and older individuals from a role identity theory perspective (Leedahl et al., 2017; van Ingen & Wilson, 2017). A quantitative analysis conducted by Leedahl et al. (2017) revealed that civic engagement was significantly beneficial to the well-being of nursing home residents; the researchers suggested that nursing home residents benefit from civic participation because it can be a source of social support that gives them a sense of group membership and a role to assume during retirement. My findings help support this literature by revealing that retirement experiences are generally positive, particularly when police officers feel that they can continue to be engaged in civic duties like volunteerism.

My findings also reflect how financial security can help address barriers to retirement and ease the transition experience into retirement. Evidence presented in Chapter 2 showed that many retirees hire financial advisors to help them plan and enact their financial transition into retirement (Cooper et al., 2018; van Ingen & Wilson, 2017). Some retirees, however, experience significant negative ramifications as a result of hiring someone who is either poorly trained or has malicious intent. Advisors may intentionally choose ill-advised financial management options with higher fees to their own benefit. While financial factors were not mentioned by participants in this study to the same extent as was reflected in Chapter 2, it was clear that finances can be both a facilitator of, and barrier to, an effective transitioning experience. Consideration of finances appears to be an important component in the support of law enforcement professionals as they retire, and this factor may be combined with civic engagement opportunities to help reduce the potential for negative psychosocial outcomes in retirement.

With respect to mental health, my findings also support literature presented in Chapter 2. Specifically, researchers such as Rhee et al. (2016) found involuntary retirement is associated with mental health problems as a result of less perceived control of the retirees' finances. Moreover, involuntary retirement among law enforcement officers can result in low moods and feelings of isolation and abandonment that can negatively affect their self-report of life satisfaction (Cameron & Griffiths, 2016). This perception of control in retirement appears to be an important component of the promotion of a positive experience in transitioning from the professional environment.

The fact that retirees primarily reported positive experiences in retirement was in alignment with some of the literature presented in Chapter 2 as well. Specifically, literature in Chapter 2 showed that retirees generally experience positive emotions and well-being during retirement, often having better self-reported mental health perceptions compared to individuals who are still in the workforce (Syse et al., 2015). The experience of positive emotions individually in retirement may serve as a barrier because latent psychosocial health issues may begin to manifest as law enforcement professionals progress in their retirement. These professionals may experience a sense of identity loss that does not become apparent until several years into retirement. Additionally, police officers are also known for avoiding mental health services as a result of their fear of being stigmatized (Bullock

& Garland, 2017). Addressing these psychosocial issues during retirement in a qualitative study is necessary in order to gain a deeper understanding of how police officers can be better prepared for retirement (Bullock et al., 2018). Furthermore, there appears to be a need to assess the psychosocial experiences of retirement longitudinally and not just at the outset of retirement, as negative effects associated with identity loss may not begin to manifest for several years.

The second research question was, "What factors positively impact the retirement of police officers?" The three themes that emerged in response to RQ2 were: having more time in retirement is a positive factor, dealing with less stress is positive, and being prepared for retirement positively impacts the experience. These findings also support literature presented in Chapter 2 that demonstrated which factors appear to most contribute to a positive retirement experience. While many researchers have found positive outcomes from the retirement transition, challenges and obstacles have also been found in numerous studies (Henning et al., 2016; Syse et al., 2015). From my study, it was apparent that police officers were less inclined to report negative experiences with retirement than what has been shown in the previous literature.

These findings do appear to show that police officers in this study had proadaptive responses to retirement, which may have been a result of their preparation and support. Several studies have confirmed the finding that adaptive behaviors, including bridge employment and adopting new leisure activities, are associated with positive retirement outcomes (Henning et al., 2016). It is, however, important to note that these findings are meant to apply only to the immediate period following retirement that is characterized by a transition away from one's working role and into the role of a retiree. Most studies on general retirement or retirement among police officers report positive experiences. Thus, it is notable that among the sample of officers studied by Cameron and Griffiths (2016), all of whom retired involuntarily, more negative outcomes were reported than positive. In my study, alternative factors may have played a role in the reporting of positive experiences with retirement, such as increased financial control, civic engagement, and psychosocial support.

Police officers in this study did not report the same level of negative psychosocial experiences that has been shown in some of the previous literature presented in Chapter 2. Denial, stress, anger, and anxiety are some of the common psychological experiences of retirees during retirement (Abdulkadir et al., 2018). Stress and anxiety are also common psychological experiences among some retirees during retirement (Saraswat, 2017). Anxiety and stress during retirement are primarily as a result of a perceived loss of control in some manner, be it financial or due to the loss of one's preretirement role (Burkert & Hochfellner, 2017). Thus, my findings offer a contribution to the literature and practice by demonstrating which factors contribute to positive psychosocial experiences following retirement from law enforcement.

Preparation appears to be a key factor in determining whether retirement experiences are positive. In another recent study, Olatomide (2017) found that both preretirement counseling and family involvement had a significant and positive effects on how retirees adjusted to retirement. Gathiira et al. (2019) went even further, suggesting that participation in retirement counseling programs with a psychosocial focus could help mitigate the negative implications of participants' lack of preparedness for retirement. Among 334 working professionals representing a larger sample who participated in a retirement counseling program with a psychosocial focus, participants' preparedness for retirement was found to significantly increase following program completion (Gathiira et al., 2019). These findings offer an indication of why some police officers appear to have positive versus negative experiences as they transition into retirement.

The third research question was, "What factors negatively impact the retirement of police officers?" The three themes that emerged in response to RQ3 were: missing being a police officer negatively impacted the retirement experience, missing coworkers also negatively impacted retirement, and that there were no viewed negative impacts. This finding is somewhat novel, as much of the previous research has focused on negative outcomes associated with retirement.

Nevertheless, examples of research on this transition have revealed significantly different experiences, both positive and negative. The type of retirement one undergoes can significantly impact the trajectory of the process (Cameron & Griffiths, 2016; Rhee et al., 2016). Retirement can be voluntary, compulsory, or mandatory (Abdulkadir et al., 2018). Voluntary retirement is initiated by employees by choice. Compulsory and mandatory forms of retirement are similar but distinct; compulsory retirement is an involuntary retirement dictated by employers, while mandatory retirement occurs when employees reach a predetermined age or benchmark (Abdulkadir et al., 2018). Among older adults up to the age of 68, negative experiences transitioning to retirement and a lesser likelihood of participating in bridge employment were associated with self-reported physical limitations around age 53. Volunteer work and bridge employment were found to be more likely among individuals who performed well on tests of cognition and physical capabilities. I found civic engagement to be an important facilitator of a successful retirement experience, and volunteerism may be one way in which to promote this experience.

Additionally, police officers in this study may have been more prepared to enter retirement than what has been typically shown in the literature. According to Abdulkadir et al. (2018), preretirement counseling can lessen the likelihood of: "i. Post-retirement shock and health problems, ii. Negative stereotype ideas associated with retirement, [and] iii. Dissatisfaction with retirement and tendency to miss ones' previous job routine" (p. 15). Recently, innovative programs such as the Peers as Law Enforcement Support (PALS) program have been implemented in the United States to help law enforcement officers adequately and comfortably address personal concerns and challenges so that they do not persist through an officer's career and into retirement (Hasselt et al., 2019). Though police officers in this study did not necessarily indicate that they had engaged in formal counselling or transition programs, it did appear that they were more prepared for retirement than what has been demonstrated in the literature. There is a need to evaluate the success of such programs in future literature for reducing adverse psychosocial experiences associated with retirement.

My findings have implications for the conceptual framework that underpinned this study as well. This study was informed by the theory of continuity (Atchley, 1989) and the role theory of retirement (Mead, 1913). I found the theory of continuity to be appropriate for conceptualizing the findings of this study because of the insights gained regarding the tendency of retirees to adopt a way of life that is similar to their way of life before retirement (Atchley, 1989). My selection of role theory was also appropriate for analyzing the experiences of police officers because of the importance placed on the perspectives of individuals in understanding their experiences and adjustments during retirement. The main tenet of the continuity theory is that retirees are more likely to experience psychological well-being when they are able to preserve a lifestyle that is somewhat similar to their life before retirement (Atchley, 1989). Through adaptive choices, middle-aged police officers appear to be preserving and maintaining both internal and external structures that are tied to their past experiences and social environments. Based on continuity theory, change, such as retirement, is seen as related to the perceived past of a person, facilitating the continuance of behaviors and psychological beliefs that are central to one's preretirement functioning (Atchley, 1989). One reason that police officers in my study reported primarily positive experiences was that they were able to continue civic engagement through volunteerism in retirement.

My findings also support literature than has used continuity theory to conceptualize retirement. For example, continuity theory has been used as framework for other studies involving retirement (Henning et al., 2016; Oleksiyenko & Życzyńska-Ciołek, 2018). Another theoretical component of the study's conceptual framework was role identity theory, wherein the concepts of self and the mind are considered the foundation (Mead, 1913). Specifically, roles are developed through social interaction as perceived and interpreted by individuals as the actors (Mead, 1913). Role theory has also been used as a framework for understanding the psychosocial experiences of retirees and older individuals (Henning et al., 2016; Leedahl et al., 2017; van Ingen & Wilson, 2017). It was evident from the findings of this study that police officers were able to maintain their roles in retirement through civic engagement and volunteerism. The following section contains a discussion of limitations that were present in the research design and methodology and which may have influenced the trustworthiness of the findings.

Limitations of the Study

As with all qualitative, phenomenological studies, some limitations were present that may have influenced trustworthiness. The limitations of the study related to design and methodological weaknesses included subjectivity of the data and the relative complexity of the data analysis procedure. In order to address these limitations, I aimed to strictly follow the guidelines set by Smith (2014) about interpretive phenomenological analysis. Nevertheless, there were still some limitations inherent in this design and methodology that warrant consideration.

Specifically, there were some limitations associated with transferability and dependability. Limitations of transferability and dependability included the inability to generalize the findings to all retired police officers because of the small sample size and nonrandomized sampling method. Given the experiential differences in voluntary and nonvoluntary retirement (Cameron & Griffiths, 2016; Rhee et al., 2016), the results of the study may not be transferable to police officers who retired either mandatorily or compulsorily. The results may not be transferrable outside of this study if not enough similarities exist in terms of the sample composition, characteristics of the context, or the nature of the phenomenon.

Researcher bias also could have also influenced the research findings in terms of not being able to successfully set aside preconceived ideas about the psychosocial experiences of retired police officers. The interpretative nature of the data analytic approach inherently requires subjectivity on the part of the research. I addressed this potential bias by engaging in the psychological process of bracketing during data collection and analysis. According to Tufford and Newman (2012), bracketing in qualitative studies has the potential to prevent the negative influence of preconceptions that could pollute the quality of the study process. Some interpretations were necessary, however, and bias could have influenced the manner in which the themes were generated in this research. The following section contains a discussion of recommendations based on the limitations in this study.

Recommendations

Based on these limitations, several recommendations can be made regarding methodological choices taken in subsequent research, as well as to inform practice related to counselling and psychosocial support for police officers who are transitioning into retirement. First, with respect to methodology, I recommend that steps be taken to address the threats to trustworthiness that were identified above. Specifically, I recommend that studies that use larger sample sizes and random sampling methods be implemented in order to improve the generalizability of the findings. Additionally, quantitative studies and samples from other settings and contexts would help facilitate a determination of the extent to which the themes identified in this research are generalizable to the larger population of police offers entering retirement.

A logical extension of these findings is to conduct interventions that are designed to prevent negative psychosocial experiences in retiring law enforcement professionals and to improve the transitioning process. Through the application of continuity theory and retirement role theory, positive interventions that encompass the range of factors that may pro- duce stress may prevent averse psychosocial outcomes through well-de- signed intervention and case studies. Additionally, I recommend that police officers be screened as they enter retirement to assess any psycho- social risk factors that warrant counselling or intervention as they leave the professional environment. Transitioning programs, civic engagement, and financial counselling may all be important ways to provide support to police officers as they transition from the professional workforce and into their retirement.

With respect to policy, I recommend that law enforcement agencies in the United States implement programs that are designed to improve the transition process from the professional environment to retirement. Doing so will have a positive impact on law enforcement professionals and may help reduce the need for long-term mental health care and/or medication associated with mental health issues like anxiety and depression. Furthermore, support programs and strategies that allow for civic engagement should be included in law enforcement policy in order to offer mental and social support to police officers. The following section contains a discussion of implications of the findings of this study for research, theory, and practice.

Implications

My findings offer many contributions to the understanding of police officers' experiences with retirement, including barriers to transitioning and factors which determine a successful transitional experience. Perhaps the most significant contribution of this phenomenological research study is that advancing knowledge in the discipline includes the enhanced understanding of the different psychosocial challenges that retired police officers experience during retirement. I was also be able to understand the relevance of roles and transitions during retirement. The information I obtained from the semistructured interviews helps to address a gap in research on the lived experience of police officers during retirement given that previous research has primarily been lacking in in-depth details of this phenomenon.

Another significant contribution from this study that advances practice and policy includes the potential to improve preretirement programs for police officers that better prepare them for their psychosocial adjustment. This research study could also be instrumental in the development of interventions that can help police officers become more positively adjusted in their retirements based on a deeper understanding of their psychosocial experiences. As a result of the findings of this research study, leaders of police departments could be encouraged to be more proactive with their assistance towards police officers who are about to retire.

The potential implications for positive social change that are consistent with and bounded by the scope of my study include better psychosocial adjustment of retired police officers. When retired police officers are more adjusted to their retirement, common psychosocial problems such as denial, social isolation, stress, anger, and anxiety may be lessened or avoided (Abdulkadir et al., 2018). The workload of the healthcare systems may be lessened if police departments are both preventive and proactive in putting programs into place that facilitate better transition to retirement among their police officers. The results of the study could also directly benefit the participants by allowing them to learn more about themselves, thus contributing to positive social change on the individual level in their own communities. The following section concludes the chapter.

Conclusion

The purpose of this chapter was to provide a discussion of findings and conclusions that can be drawn based on their alignment with the literature and theory presented in Chapter 2. An interpretation of the findings was presented first, followed by limitations that may have influenced trustworthiness. Findings from this study helped to extend literature presented in Chapter 2 regarding the psychosocial experiences of police officers as they transition into retirement. There were some limitations to trustworthiness identified in this study, primarily regarding the small sample size, the lack of random sampling, and the interpretive nature of the analytical process that may have been exposed to bias on the part of the research.

I then made recommendations for future practice and research. In addition to addressing the limitations that were identified, I also recommended that screening practices be implemented to assess psychosocial risk, as well as to provide programs that enable continued civic engagement, financial control, and social support. Each of these strategies could help police officers feel they are continuing their roles as civic servants, have control over their finances, and are connected to their social identities as law enforcement professionals.

I then drew implications were for positive social change as well as methodological issues, theory, and practice. With respect to positive social change, my findings have the potential to improve the retirement experiences of law enforcement professionals via the identification of psychosocial risk factors and the provision of support for police officers who may suffer from role conflicts, trauma, anxiety, and depression as they enter retirement. Regarding theory, these findings help demonstrate how continuity theory and retirement role theory offer an effective conceptualization of the retirement experience for law enforcement professionals and may be used to guide interventions that prevent negative psychosocial outcomes. Regarding practice, my findings may help improve retirement experiences for police officers by identifying risk factors and preventing the manifestation of mental health issues like depression and anxiety. This concludes Chapter 5 and the dissertation.

References

Abdulkadir, A., Rasaq, A. O., & Gafar, I. (2018). Psychological effects of retirement of retirees: Implications for counselling. *Cypriot Journal of Educational Sciences*, *13*(1), 15–22. https://doi.org/10.18844/cjes.v13i1.3365

Agahi, N., Kelfve, S., Hassing, L., Johansson, B., & Lindwall, M. (2018). Trajectories of alcohol consumption in relation to retirement transition in Sweden. *Innovation in Aging, 2*(1), 388. https://doi.org/10.1093/geroni/igy023.1448

Amankwaa, L. (2016). Creating protocols for trustworthiness in qualitative research. *Journal of Cultural Diversity, 23*(3), 121–127. https://web.b.ebscohost.com/

Atchley, R. C. (1989). A continuity theory of normal aging. *Gerontologist, 29,* 183–190. https://doi.org/10.1093/geront/29.2.183

Bazeley, P., & Jackson, K. (2013). *Qualitative data analysis with NVivo.* SAGE. https://doi.org/10.1080/14780887.2014.992750

Beck, V., & Williams, G. (2015). The (performance) management of retirement and the limits of individual choice. *Work, Employment and Society, 29,* 267–277. https://doi.org/10.1177/ 0950017014559963

Black, A., McCabe, D., & McConnell, N. (2013). Ten years on, living with the 'psychological troubles': Retired police officers in Northern Ireland. *Irish Journal of Psychology, 34*(2), 93–108. https://doi.org/10.1080/03033910.2013.809664

Bowler, R. M., Kornblith, E. S., Li, J., Adams, S. W., Gocheva, V. V., Schwarzer, R., & Cone, J. E. (2016). Police officers who responded to 9/11: Comorbidity of PTSD, depression, and anxiety 10–11 years later. *American Journal of Industrial Medicine, 59*(6), 425–436. https://doi.org/10.1002/ajim.22588

Bracken-Scally, M., McGilloway, S., & Mitchell, J. T. (2016). Retirement policies and support for emergency service personnel: The transition to retirement. *Canadian Journal on Aging, 35*(2), 161–174. https://doi.org/1017/S0714980816000210

Bresler, L. (2008). Research as experience and the experience of research: Mutual shaping in the arts and in qualitative inquiry. *Learning Landscapes, 2*(1), 267–281. https://doi.org/10.36510/learnland.v2i1.288

Bullock, K., Fielding, J., & Hieke, G. (2018). Retiring from the police service in England and Wales: A multi-dimensional perspective. *Ageing & Society, 40*(1), 1–24. https://doi.org/10.1017/S0144686X18000818P

Bullock, K., & Garland, J. (2017). Police officers, mental (ill-) health and spoiled identity. *Criminology and Criminal Justice, 18*(2), 1–17. https://doi.org/10.1177/1748895817695856

Bullock, K., Garland, J., & Coupar, F. (2019). Police officer transitions to retirement in the United Kingdom: Social identity, social support, and (in) justice. *Policing and Society, 10*, 1–15. https://doi.org/10.1080/10439463.2019.1664522

Burkert, C., & Hochfellner, D. (2017). Employment trajectories beyond retirement. *Journal of Aging & Social Policy, 29*(2), 143–167. https://doi.org/10.1080/0895942 0.2016.1213092

Cameron, T. M., & Griffiths, A. (2016). The impact of involuntary retirement on senior police officers. *Policing, 11*(1), 52–61. https://doi.org/10.1093/police/paw020

Chan, Z. C. Y., Fung, Y., & Chien, W. (2013). Bracketing in phenomenology: Only undertaken in the data collection and analysis process. *Qualitative Report, 18*(30). https://doi.org/10.46743/2160-3715/2013.1486

Charman, S. (2017). *Police socialisation, identity and culture: Becoming blue.* Springer. https://doi.org/10.1007/978-3-319-63070-0_1

Connelly, L. M. (2016). Trustworthiness in qualitative research. *Medsurg Nursing, 25*(6), 435–437. https://go.gale.com/

Cooper, J., Minney, A., & Haqqani, A. (2018). *Retirement really is different* [Position paper]. Challenger. https://www.challenger.com.au/-/media/challenger/ documents/thought-leadership/Retirement-Really-Is-Different-Position-Paper.pdf

Corpuz, R. R. (2020). Shared stories of retired police officers on the current issues in the police service and retirement woes. *SSRN.* https://papers.ssrn.com/sol3/ papers.cfm?abstract_id=3560205

Dingemans, E., & Henkens, K. (2017). Working after retirement and its relationship with life satisfaction. *Innovation in Aging, 1*(1), 62. https://doi.org/10.1093/geroni/igx004.254

Dingemans, E., Henkens, K., & Van Solinge, H. (2017). Working retirees in Europe: Individual and societal determinants. *Work, Employment and Society, 31*(6), 972–991. https://doi.org/10.1177/0950017016664677

Eagers, J., Franklin, R. C., Yau, M. K., & Broome, K. (2018). Pre-retirement job and the work-to-retirement occupational transition process in Australia: A review. *Australian Occupational Therapy Journal, 65*(4), 314–328. https://doi.org/10.1111/1440-1630.12452

Fadila, D. E. & Alam, R. R., (2016). Factors affecting adjustment to retirement among retirees' elderly persons. *Journal of Nursing Education and Practice, 6*(8). https://doi.org/10.5430/jnep.v6n8p112

Fenge, L., & Lee, S. (2018). Understanding the risks of financial scams as part of elder abuse prevention. *British Journal of Social Work, 48*(4), 906–923. https://doi.org/10.1093/bjsw/bcy037

Flory, J., & Emanuel, E. (2004). Interventions to improve research participants' understanding in informed consent for research: A systematic review. *Jama, 292*(13), 1593–1601. https://doi.org/10.1001/jama.292.13.1593

Francis, J. J., Johnston, M., Robertson, C., Glidewell, L., Entwistle, V., Eccles, M. P., & Grimshaw, J. M. (2010). What is an adequate sample size? Operationalising data saturation for theory-based interview studies. *Psychology and Health, 25*(10), 1229–1245. https://doi.org/10.1080/08870440903194015

Fusch, P. I., & Ness, L. R. (2015). Are we there yet? Data saturation in qualitative research. *The Qualitative Report, 20*(9), 1408–1416. https://doi.org/10.46743/2160-3715/2015.2281

Gathiira, T. G., Muathe, S. M., & Kilika, J. M. (2019). Psychosocial programmes and employees' retirement preparedness: Empirical evidence from the educational sector in Kenya. *International Journal of Business Administration, 10*(2), 82–95. https://doi.org/10.5430/ijba.v10n2p82

Glaser, B. G., & Strauss, A. L. (2017). *Discovery of grounded theory: Strategies for qualitative research.* Routledge. https://doi.org/10.4324/9780203793206

Haslam, C., Lam, B. C., Branscombe, N. R., Steffens, N. K., Haslam, S. A., Cruwys, T., Fong, P., & Ball, T. C. (2018). Adjusting to life in retirement: The protective role of new group memberships and identification as a retiree. *European Journal of Work and Organizational Psychology, 27*(6), 822–839. https://doi.org/10.1080/1359432X.2018.1538127

Hasselt, V. B., Klimley, K. E., Rodriguez, S., Themis-Fernandez, M., Henderson, S. N., & Schneider, B. A. (2019). Peers as law enforcement support (PALS): An early prevention program. *Aggression and Violent Behavior, 48*, 1–5. https://doi.org/10.1016/j.avb.2019.05.004

Hellström, T. (2008). Transferability and naturalistic generalization: New generalizability concepts for social science or old wine in new bottles? *Quality & Quantity, 42*(3), 321–337. https://doi.org/10.1007/s11135-006-9048-0

Henning, G., Lindwall, M., & Johansson, B. (2016). Continuity in well-being in the transition to retirement. *GeroPsych, 29*, 225–237. https://doi.org/10.1024/1662-9647/a000155

Hope, J. (2017). Recognize challenges of mental illness in law enforcement, support officers seeking help. *Campus Security Report, 14*(5), 6–7. https://doi.org/10.1002/casr.30300

Jootun, D., McGhee, G., & Marland, G. R. (2009). Reflexivity: Promoting rigour in qualitative research. *Nursing Standard, 23*(23), 42–46. https://doi.org/10.7748/ns2009.02.23.23.42.c6800

Kalenkoski, C. M., & McCarty, S. H. (2019). In or out or somewhere in between? The determinants of gradual retirement. *Journal of Family and Economic Issues, 42*(2), 387–394. https://doi.org/10.1007/s10834-020-09734-4

Karlin, N. J., Weil, J., & Salem, M. B. (2019). Social Support, Retirement Resources, and the Gendered Experiences of Aging for Tunisian Older Adults. *Journal of Gerontological Social Work, 62*(5), 564–577. https://doi.org/10.1080/01634372.2019.1610132

Kirschman, E. (2018). *I love a cop: What police families need to know.* Guilford Press. https://www.guilford.com/books/I-Love-a-Cop/Ellen-Kirschman/9781462533855

Korstjens, I., & Moser, A. (2018). Series: Practical guidance to qualitative research. Part 4: Trustworthiness and publishing. *European Journal of General Practice, 24*(1), 120–124. https://doi.org/10.1080/13814788.2017.1375092

Lam, B. C., Haslam, C., Haslam, S. A., Steffens, N. K., Cruwys, T., Jetten, J.,
& Yang, J. (2018). Multiple social groups support adjustment to retirement
across cultures. *Social Science & Medicine, 208*, 200–208.
https://doi.org/10.1016/j.socscimed.2018.05.049

Landon, M. G., & Ritz, J. M. (2016). Motivational factors that influence retirement
contentment. *Research & Reviews: Journal of Social Sciences, 2*(2), 1–22.
https://www.rroij.com/social-sciences.php

Leedahl, S. N., Sellon, A. M., & Gallopyn, N. (2017). Factors predicting civic
engagement among older adult nursing home residents. *Activities, Adaptation
& Aging, 41*(3), 197–219. https://doi.org/10.1080/01924788.2017.1310581

Leppma, M., Mnatsakanova, A., Sarkisian, K., Scott, O., Adjeroh, L., Andrew, M. E.,
Violanti, J. M., & McCanlies, E. C. (2018). Stressful life events and posttraumatic
growth among police officers: A cross-sectional study. *Stress and Health, 34*(1),
175–186. https://doi.org/10.1002/smi.2772

MacKenzie, K. (2017). A case for incorporating financial wellness into your
retirement planning practice. *Journal of Financial Service Professionals, 71*(3).
https://web.b.ebscohost.com/

Madden, R. (2017). *Being ethnographic: A guide to the theory and practice of
ethnography.* SAGE. https://doi.org/10.4135/9781529716689

Marchand, A., Nadeau, C., Beaulieu-Prévost, D., Boyer, R., & Martin, M. (2015).
Predictors of posttraumatic stress disorder among police officers: A prospective
study. *Psychological Trauma: Theory, Research, Practice, and Policy, 7*(3), 212–212.
https://doi.org/10.1037/a0038780

Mazumdar, B., Warren, A., & Brown, T. C. (2017). Outcomes of bridge employment:
A psychological contract theory perspective. *Academy of Management Annual
Meeting Proceedings, 2017*(1). https://doi.org/10.5465/AMBPP.2017.15589abstract

Mead, G. H. (1913). The social self. *Journal of Philosophy, Psychology and Scientific
Methods, 10*(14), 374–380. https://doi.org/10.2307/2012910

Moustakas, C. (1994). *Phenomenological research methods.* SAGE.
https://doi.org/10.4135/9781412995658

NCSL. (n.d.). *State governments' public safety retirement plans.* https://www.ncsl.org/
research/fiscal-policy/state-retirement-plans-public-safety-tables.aspx

Nho, S. M., & Kim, E. A. (2017). Factors influencing post-traumatic stress disorder in crime scene investigators. *Journal of Korean Academy of Nursing, 47*(1), 39–48. https://doi.org/10.4040/jkan.2017.47.1.39

Noy, C. (2008). Sampling knowledge: The hermeneutics of snowball sampling in qualitative research. *International Journal of Social Research Methodology, 11*(4), 327–344. https://doi.org/10.1080/13645570701401305

Olatomide, O. O. (2017). Impacts of pre-retirement guidance and family involvement on retirement adjustment of retirees in Nigeria. *Bulgarian Journal of Science & Education Policy, 11*(2), 246–266. http://bjsep.org/

Oleksiyenko, O., & Życzyńska-Ciołek, D. (2018). Structural determinants of workforce participation after retirement in Poland. *Journal of Population Ageing, 11*(1), 83–103. https://doi.org/10.1007/s12062-017-9213-3

Onijigin, E. O. (2020). The influence of retirement counselling on retirement plan among civil servants in Ekiti State. *Online Submission, 1*(2), 1–2. https://www.easij.com/

Oude-Mulders, J. (2019). Attitudes about working beyond normal retirement age: The role of mandatory retirement. *Journal of Aging & Social Policy, 32*(2), 1–17. https://doi.org/10.1080/08959420.2018.1563473

Palinkas, L. A., Horwitz, S. M., Green, C. A., Wisdom, J. P., Duan, N., & Hoagwood, K. (2015). Purposeful sampling for qualitative data collection and analysis in mixed method implementation research. *Administration and Policy in Mental Health and Mental Health Services Research, 42*(5), 533–544. https://doi.org/10.1007/s10488-013-0528-y

Pandey, S. C., & Patnaik, S. (2014). Establishing reliability and validity in qualitative inquiry: A critical examination. *Jharkhand Journal of Development and Management Studies, 12*(1), 5743–5753. https://www.xiss.ac.in/JJDMS/publication.php

Price, M. (2017). Psychiatric disability in law enforcement officers. *Behavioral Sciences & the Law, 35*(2), 113–123. https://doi.org/10.1002/bsl.2278

Rabionet, S. E. (2011). How I learned to design and conduct semi-structured interviews: An ongoing and continuous journey. *Qualitative Report, 16*(2), 563–66. https://doi.org/10.46743/2160-3725/2011.1070

Reisi, A., Fathi Ashtiani, A., Salimi, S. H., & Rabie, M. (2017). Considering the general health of retired high rank police officers and providing some solutions to reduce their psychological problem during retirement. *Journal of Police Medicine, 5*(5), 351–360. http://jpmed.ir/en

Rhee, M. K., Mor Barak, M. E., & Gallo, W. T. (2016). Mechanisms of the effect of involuntary retirement on older adults' self-rated health and mental health. *Journal of Gerontological Social Work, 59*(1), 35–55. https://doi.org/10.1080/01634372.2015.1128504

Saraswat, A. G. (2017). Stress and Satisfaction attained by retirees through bridge employment in service sector. *International Journal of Scientific Research and Management, 5*(7), 6521–6523. https://doi.org/10.18535/ijsrm/v5i7.91

Shiba, K., Kondo, N., Kondo, K., & Kawachi, I. (2017). Retirement and mental health: Does social participation mitigate the association? A fixed-effects longitudinal analysis. *BMC Public Health, 17*(1), 526–535. https://doi.org/10.1186/s12889-017-4427-0

Shin, O., Park, S., Kwak, M., & Kang, J. (2018). The profiles of vulnerabilities among retirees in USA. *Innovation in Aging, 2*, 1005–1005. https://doi.org/10.1093/geroni/igy031.3715

Simon, M. K., & Goes, J. (2013). Assumptions, limitations, delimitations, and scope of the study. dissertationrecipes.com

Spraggins, N. (2019). *Preparing for life after a police career* [Leadership White Paper, Leadership Command College]. Bill Blackwood Law Enforcement Management Institute of Texas. https://shsu-ir.tdl.org/bitstream/handle/20.500.11875/2660/1881.pdf?sequence=1&isAllowed=y

Stafford, M., Cooper, R., Cadar, D., Carr, E., Murray, E., Richards, M., Stansfeld, S., Zaninotto, P., Head, J., & Kuh, D. (2017). Physical and cognitive capability in mid-adulthood as determinants of retirement and extended working life in a British cohort study. *Scandinavian Journal of Work, Environment, & Health, 43*(1), 15–23. https://doi.org/10.5271/sjweh.3589

Steinkopf, B. L., Hakala, K. A., & Van Hasselt, V. B. (2015). Motivational interviewing: Improving the delivery of psychological services to law enforcement. *Professional Psychology: Research and Practice, 46*(5), 348–354. https://doi.org/10.1037/pro0000042

Suri, H. (2011). Purposeful sampling in qualitative research synthesis. *Qualitative Research Journal, 11*(2), 63–75. https://doi.org/10.3316/QRJ1102063

Syse, A., Veenstra, M., Furunes, T., Mykletun, R. J., & Solem, P. E. (2015). Changes in health and health behavior associated with retirement. *Journal of aging and Health, 29*(1), 99–127. https://doi.org/10.1177/0898264315624906

Topa, G., Lunceford, G., & Boyatzis, R. E. (2018). Financial planning for retirement: A psychosocial perspective. *Frontiers in Psychology, 8,* 2338. https://doi. org/10.3389/fpsyg.2017.02338/full

Topa, G., & Valero, E. (2017). Preparing for retirement: How self-efficacy and resource threats contribute to retirees' satisfaction, depression, and losses. *European Journal of Work and Organizational Psychology, 26*(6), 811–827. https://doi.org/10.1080/1359432X.2017.1375910

Tufford, L., & Newman, P. (2012). Bracketing in qualitative research. *Qualitative Social Work, 11*(1), 80–96. https://doi.org/10.1177/1473325010368316

Umukoro, O. S., & Adejuwon, G. A. (2017). Mediatory role of social support on psychological antecedents of retirement satisfaction among police retirees in Nigeria. *International Journal of Caring Sciences, 10*(3), 1402–1409. http://www.internationaljournalofcaringsciences.org

van Ingen, E., & Wilson, J. (2017). I volunteer, therefore I am? Factors affecting volunteer role identity. *Nonprofit and Voluntary Sector Quarterly, 46*(1), 29–46. https://doi.org/10.1177/0899764016659765

van den Bogaard, L., Henkens, K., & Kalmijn, M. (2016). Retirement as a relief? The role of physical job demands and psychological job stress for effects of retirement on self-rated health. *European Sociological Review, 32*(2), 295–306. https://doi.org/10.1093/esr/jcv135

Violanti, J. M., Owens, S. L., McCanlies, E., Fekedulegn, D., & Andrew, M. E. (2018). Law enforcement suicide: A review. *Policing: An International Journal of Police Strategies & Management, 42,* 141–164. https://doi.org/10.1108/PIJPSM-05-2017-0061

Wang, K., & Bishop, N. J. (2019). Social support and monetary resources as protective factors against food insecurity among older Americans: Findings from a health and retirement study. *Food Security, 11*(4), 929–939. https://doi.org/10.1007/s12571-019-00945-8

Wang, M., & Wanberg, C. R. (2017). 100 years of applied psychology research on individual careers: From career management to retirement. *Journal of Applied Psychology, 102*(3), 546. https://doi.org/10.1037/ap10000143

Washburn, R. (2018). *Preparing police officers for retirement: Financial and emotional wellness* [Leadership White Paper]. The Bill Blackwood Law Enforcement Management Institute of Texas. https://shsu-ir.tdl.org/bitstream/handle/20.500.11875/2522/1831.pdf?sequence=1&isAllowed=y

Wetzel, M., Huxhold, O., & Tesch-Romer, C. (2016). Transition into retirement affects life satisfaction: Short-and long-term development depends on last labor market status and education. *Social Indicators Research, 125*(3), 991–1009. https://doi.org/10.1007/s11205- 015-0862-4

Wilson, E., Kenny, A., & Dickson-Swift, V. (2018). Ethical challenges of community based participatory research: Exploring researchers' experience. *International Journal of Social Research Methodology, 21*(1), 7–24. https://doi.org/10.1080/13645579.2017.1296714

Yin, R. K. (2017). *Case study research and applications: Design and methods.* SAGE. https://us.sagepub.com/en-us/nam/case-study-research-and-applications/book250150#contents

Yu, S., Brackbill, R. M., Locke, S., Stellman, S. D., & Gargano, L. M. (2016). Impact of 9/11-related chronic conditions and PTSD comorbidity on early retirement and job loss among World Trade Center disaster rescue and recovery workers. *American Journal of Industrial Medicine, 59*(9), 731–741. https://doi.org/10.1002/ajim.22640

Appendix A: Interview Guide

1. How would you describe your transition to retirement?

2. How would you describe your psychological health during your retirement?

3. How would you describe your social experiences during your retirement?

4. What challenges have you encountered during retirement?

5. What factors positively impact your retirement?

6. What factors negatively impact your retirement?

7. What other relevant information that you can share that we have not yet discussed?

Appendix B: Eligibility Check

1. Are you a retired police officer?

2. Are you currently residing in the northeastern region of the United States?

3. Are you willing to participate in Skype/Zoom interview?

Appendix C: Informed Consent

The purpose of this phenomenological study is to explore how retired police officers perceive their psychosocial experiences during their retirements and the positive and negative factors that impact their retirements. The researcher is inviting retired police officers in the northeastern region of the United States to participate in the study. This form is part of a process called "informed consent" to allow you to understand this study before deciding whether to take part.

This study is being conducted by a researcher named Steven Kelsey, who is a doctoral student at Walden University.

Background Information:
The purpose of this phenomenological study is to explore how retired police officers perceive their psychosocial experiences during their retirement and the positive and negative factors that impact their retirement

Procedures:
If you agree to be in this study, you will be asked to:
- Participate in a Zoom/Skype interview session (less than 1 hour)
- Review and validate interview responses (approx. 30 minutes)

Here are the interview questions:

1. How would you describe your transition to retirement?

2. How would you describe your psychological health during your retirement?

3. How would you describe your social experiences during your retirement?

4. What challenges have you encountered during retirement?

5. What factors positively impact your retirement?

6. What factors negatively impact your retirement?

7. What other relevant information that you can share that we have not yet discussed?

Voluntary Nature of the Study:

This study is voluntary. Everyone will respect your decision of whether or not you choose to be in the study. No one will treat you differently if you decide not to be in the study. If you decide to join the study now, you can still change your mind later. You may stop at any time.

Risks and Benefits of Being in the Study:

Being in this type of study involves some risk of the minor discomforts that can be encountered in daily life, such as fatigue and stress. Being in this study would not pose risk to your safety or wellbeing.

As a result of the findings of this research study, leaders of police departments could be encouraged to be more proactive with their assistance towards police officers who are about to retire.

Payment:

There will be no payment given for participating in the study.

Privacy:

Any information you provide will be kept confidential. The researcher will not use your personal information for any purposes outside of this research project. Also, the researcher will not include your name or anything else that could identify you in the study reports. Data will be kept secure by using aggregate or pseudonyms for presentation. All data will be stored in a password protected computer and a locked filing cabinet in the private office of the researcher. Data will be kept for a period of at least 5 years, as required by the university.

Contacts and Questions:

You may ask any questions you have now. Or if you have questions later, you may contact the researcher via _____@waldenu.edu.

Walden University's approval number for this study is **IRB will enter approval number here** and it expires on **IRB will enter expiration date**.

The researcher will give you a copy of this consent form. You may opt to print or save a copy.

Obtaining Your Consent

If you feel you understand the study well enough to make a decision about it, and if you agree to participate in the audio-recorded interview session, please sign below.

Participant's Name _____

Signature _____